Workbook

MORE! 3

Gerngross · Puchta
Holzmann · Lewis-Jones · Stranks

HELBLING

General course

Liebe Schülerin, lieber Schüler!

Neben vielen Übungen, mithilfe derer du deine Kenntnisse der englischen Sprache erweitern und festigen kannst, findest du im Workbook am Ende jeder Unit auch eine Auflistung des Lernvokabulars, also der wichtigsten Wörter und Phrasen aus der jeweiligen Unit.

Diese Wortlisten sind in zwei Abschnitte unterteilt:

1. Word File

Unter dieser Überschrift werden jene Wörter und Ausdrücke nochmals aufgelistet, die im mit *Vocabulary* bezeichneten Abschnitt einer Unit im Student's Book eingeführt und in den darauf folgenden Aktivitäten geübt werden.

2. MORE Words and Phrases

In diesem Abschnitt findest du die wichtigsten Wörter aus der jeweiligen Unit im Student's Book. Sie sind in der Reihenfolge aufgelistet, wie sie im Student's Book vorkommen, und zur leichteren Orientierung auch mit der jeweiligen Nummer einer Aktivität aus dem Student's Book gekennzeichnet: ❶, ❷ usw.

Wichtig: Jene Wörter und Wortgruppen, die fett gedruckt sind, kommen im Alltag ganz häufig vor. Du solltest sie wirklich gut beherrschen!

Zusatzinformation: Der Vollständigkeit halber soll auch noch darauf hingewiesen werden, dass es natürlich viele andere Wörter gibt, die im Student's Book eingeführt werden, die aber im Lernvokabular im Workbook nicht vorkommen. Der Grund dafür ist, dass sie im Alltag nicht so häufig gebraucht werden und daher nicht zum eigentlichen Lernvokabular gehören. Du findest sie alle – alphabetisch gereiht – in der Nachschlagliste am Ende deines Student's Book. Mithilfe dieser Liste kannst du schnell die Bedeutung neu vorgekommener Wörter nachschlagen.

Noch ein Tipp!

Wer eine Sprache gut beherrschen möchte, sollte darauf achten, dass sein Wortschatz ständig wächst. Das heißt aber auch, dass man schon gelernte Wörter regelmäßig wiederholen muss. Geh deshalb immer wieder die Wortlisten am Ende der Units in den Workbooks der 1. und 2. Klasse durch – du solltest dir davon möglichst alle gut merken!

Contents

Zeichenerklärung

1 – Diese Übung enthält wichtige Inhalte und sollte nicht ausgelassen werden.

2 – Diese Übung kann bei Zeitmangel im Sinne eines "Fast track" durch die Unit ohne Probleme ausgelassen werden.

3 CHOICES – Bei dieser Übung stehen dir zwei Varianten zur Verfügung.

G – Grammar

SB p. 15 – Diese Übung passt zur angegebenen Seite im Student's Book (auf Seite 15).

CD4 1 – Dazu gibt es eine Tonaufnahme auf CD.
(Obere Zahl: CD Nummer / Untere Zahl: Tracknummer)

Zu dieser Übung gibt es eine Audioaufnahme, welche über ein Smartphone oder Tablet abgespielt werden kann. Zusätzlich findest du die Audioaufnahme auch im Internet (www.helbling-ezone.com).

Reading

1 **Read the story.**

The charity concert

We are a great band – the *Fab Four*. There is Carolyn. She's our brilliant singer. There is Mark on the electric guitar, Adrian on the saxophone and I'm Larissa. I play the drums.

I think we're a good band, and we were doing really well. But then one day Josh spoke to me, and everything changed. Josh is great with computers, you know. He's also a very nice guy. I really like him.

So Josh said, "I've got an idea. The computers at our school are so old and slow. Why don't you, the *Fab Four*, do a charity concert? We can invite parents, uncles and aunts. We can ask them to give us money. With the money we can buy new computers for the school."
I didn't want to say no, so I said, "I'll discuss it with the band."

At the next band practice I told my friends about Josh's idea. Carolyn and Mark were happy, but Adrian wasn't. "That's not a charity concert," he shouted. "Charity is about people. It's not about computers. A charity concert for some poor children, that's OK, but for new computers? No way!"

Mark liked the idea of a concert to buy computers. Adrian got very angry. He stood up and left.

Was this the end of our band? No, it wasn't. Josh and I talked about it. "Let's make a plan," we said. "Let's organise a concert. Let's buy computers with half of the money. Let's give the other half of the money to the children's home down the road."

Adrian agreed. We had two fantastic concerts. Why two concerts? Because we sold so many tickets. The room wasn't big enough and not everybody could get a ticket for the first show. So we played another concert. In the end we had the money for twelve computers. And we wrote two new hits – "Computer Crazy" and "Everyone's Happy Now".

SB p. 8, 9 10

2 How many of these tasks can you do?

Circle T (*True*) or F (*False*).

1 In the band, there are two boys and two girls. (T) / F

2 Mark is the guitarist. (T) / F

3 Josh, the school's computer nerd, wanted to be part of the band. T / (F)

Choose the correct answer.

4 Josh wanted the band to

- [ ] play songs about computers.
- [x] do a charity concert to raise money for computers. ✓
- [ ] give a school concert at the end of the year.

5 Larissa promised to

- [x] discuss it with the band. ✓
- [ ] help raise money for new computers.
- [ ] do a charity concert.

6 The other kids in the band

- [ ] didn't like Josh's idea.
- [x] did not all agree with Josh. ✓
- [ ] never discussed Josh's idea.

Answer the questions.

7 Why didn't Adrian like Josh's idea?

Because he wanted to give the poor kids some money. ✓

8 What plan did they come up with?

That they spent a half for computers and the other half for poor kids. ✓

9 Why did the band play two concerts?

Because they don't have enough space

3 Check your answers.

Listening

CD4 1

4 Listen to what Joanna and Lenny say about music. Tick the correct answers.

1 Joanna listens to music

- [ ] sometimes.
- [x] also in some lessons at school.
- [ ] only before she goes to bed.

2 Joanna mostly listens to

- [ ] jazz.
- [ ] hip-hop.
- [x] pop.

3 She listens to music a lot

- [x] on Spotify.
- [ ] on her dad's CDs.
- [ ] on *Spot the Pop*.

4 Joanna plays

- [ ] no instrument.
- [ ] one instrument.
- [x] two instruments.

5 Lenny plays

- [ ] no instrument.
- [x] the guitar.
- [ ] the guitar and the violin.

6 Lenny and his band play

- [ ] music by Bob Dylan and Janis Joplin.
- [x] classical music.
- [ ] dancefloor music.

7 Lenny also likes

- [ ] playing the violin.
- [x] listening to classical music.
- [ ] going to pop concerts.

8 Lenny likes to listen to music best on

- [ ] his mobile phone.
- [x] a CD player.
- [ ] an MP3-player.

SB p. 8, 9 10, 12

Essential Grammar Present simple and past simple

5 Circle the correct options to complete the text.

Shannon Green is lead guitar player with *The Sweet Lemons*. We met her on tour to ask a few questions.

Interviewer Tell us a bit about the band.

Shannon Well, there are four of us. Dan and I [1] *play / plays* the guitar. Bradley [2] *sing / sings* and plays bass and Kevin [3] *play / plays* the drums.

Interviewer Do you [4] *sing / sings*?

Shannon Sometimes.

Interviewer What kind of music does the band [5] *play / plays*?

Shannon Pop and a bit of rock.

Interviewer And [6] *do / does* you write your own music?

Shannon Well, Bradley [7] *write / writes* all the lyrics and we all [8] *write / writes* the music.

Interviewer And do you play other bands' songs?

Shannon No, we [9] *don't / doesn't*. Bradley [10] *don't / doesn't* like playing other people's music.

6 Read the text about how Shannon joined *The Sweet Lemons* and put the verbs into the past tense to complete it.

Shannon [1] ......dreamt...... (dream) of being a pop star, so she was very happy when she [2] ......got...... (get) a new guitar for her 13th birthday. There was only one problem. She [3] ......didn't know...... (not know) how to play it. She [4] ......took...... (take) some lessons and [5] ......practised...... (practise) every afternoon after school. After six months she was very good. But Shannon [6] ......didn't want...... (not want) to play on her own. She [7] ......wanted...... (want) to play in a band. There was one band at her school, *The Sweet Lemons* but they all [8] ......study...... (study) in year 6. They were all 15 and Shannon [9] ......didn't think...... (not think) they would want her.

At the end of the school year, there was a party. *The Sweet Lemons* wanted to play at the party. But the day before the show, the guitar player, Dan, [10] ......fell...... (fall) ill. The doctor [11] ......said...... (say) he had to stay in bed for a week. What [12] ......coud...... (can) they do? They [13] ......didn't...... (cannot) play without their guitarist.

Shannon [14] ......had...... (have) an idea. She [15] ......get...... (go) up to the band and [16] ......talked...... (talk) to them. The band leader Bradley was interested. Shannon played her guitar and the band thought she was very good. Bradley [17] ......asked...... (ask) her to play for them at the show. The show was a great hit and all the kids [18] ......loved...... (love) the band. Everybody [19] ......agree...... (agree) that Shannon was very good.

So what happened when Dan got better? There was only one way to keep everyone happy. *The Sweet Lemons* now have two guitarists.

SB p. 13

More Grammar Present simple and past simple

7 **Complete the dialogues with the interviewer's questions.**

~~What's your favourite band, Nigel?~~	When did you start dancing?
Did you ever buy CDs?	What did you like about *Maroon 5*?
Do you like dancing, Janice?	Do you have a favourite band to dance to?
And what do you like about *Little Mix*?	Do you listen to a lot of music, Henry?
And where do you get your music from?	

1 **Interviewer** What's your favourite band, Nigel?
Nigel That's a difficult question. For many years it was *Maroon 5*, but now it's *Little Mix*.
Interviewer And what do you like about Little Mix?
Nigel Well, their songs always had good melodies.
Interviewer What did you like about Maaroan 5?
Nigel Their lyrics are really good, and the music is more pop than rock.

2 **Interviewer** Do you like dancing, Janice
Janice Yes, I love it.
Interviewer When did you start dancing
Janice I think I started when I was five.
Interviewer Do you have a favourite band to dance to?
Janice At the moment it's *Twenty One Pilots*. They're great to dance to.

3 **Interviewer** Do you listen to a lot of music, Henry?
Henry Yeah, I listen to music as often as I can.
Interviewer And where do you get your music from?
Henry I mostly get it online. I have Spotify.
Interviewer Did you ever buy CD's?
Henry I bought a few when I was younger. And I borrowed quite a lot from an older friend. But now, as I said, I just go online.

8 **Write your answers to the interviewer's questions.**

1 What song do you like best?
....

2 And what song did you like best when you were 10?
....

3 What song do you hate most?
....

4 Where do you get your music from?
....

5 What's your favourite band?
....

6 When did you start listening to music?
....

7 Do you play an instrument? What is it and when did you start?
....

8 Where do you like listening to music?
....

9 What's the most important thing in a song for you?
....

SB p. 12, 13

Vocabulary

9 **Read the dialogue between the critic Paul Sacks and a singer on *Superstars*. Complete with the words in the box.**

give up way give training get audition make takes

Sacks Simon, Simon. Let me stop you there.

Simon What, already? I've only just started.

Sacks I don't need to hear any more. That was probably the worst [1] .... I've ever had to listen to.

Simon Oh, come on. I wasn't that bad.

Sacks Simon, yes you were. I don't know where you got the idea you could sing, but you really have to [2] .... that dream now.

Simon It was my mum. She says I have a lovely voice and that I have what it [3] .... to be a famous singer. She told me I should [4] .... this show a try.

Sacks Well, she doesn't know anything. Simon, you are not going to [5] .... it in this job. I promise you.

Simon Maybe when I've had a bit more [6] ....

Sacks No. Not with all the help in the world.

Simon Well, I think you're wrong. I know I'm on the [7] .... up.

Sacks Well, good luck and [8] .... back to me when you have your first number one.

Simon I will. You'll see. You'll be sorry one day.

10 **Complete the dialogue with the words from the box.**

famous donation take place lyrics raise performing

Seth Did you hear about the concert that'll [1] .... next Saturday?

Alice No, tell me more.

Seth They want to [2] .... some money for a new youth centre.

Alice That's a great idea but I can't go, I'm not in town next Saturday.

Seth You don't have to. You can also make a [3] .... online.

Alice OK. Who's [4] .... anyway? Anyone [5] .... ?

Seth Well, a lot of local groups. And *Skeedaddle*.

Alice Really? I love their [6] .... What a shame I'm not here.

SB p. 11

Developing speaking competencies

11 **Complete the mini-dialogues with the sentences in the box. There is one extra sentence.**

a) Me too. I didn't want it to end.
b) In my opinion, it's OK but not as good as the last film.
c) Do you think so? She was good but not brilliant.
d) I couldn't agree more. I thought it was boring.
e) Me neither. It was too loud.
f) Is it any good?
g) What did you think of the concert?

1 **Jane** I didn't really enjoy the last book we read in class. How about you?
Jack ....
Jane Let's hope the next one is better.

2 **Liz** I hope Jennifer Lawrence gets the Oscar. She was brilliant in the film.
Ollie ....
Liz No, she was absolutely fantastic.

3 **Paul** ....
Brian It was brilliant. I loved every minute of it.
Paul ....

4 **Alan** I saw the new *Star Wars* film for my birthday.
Lucy ....
Alan ....

CD4 2

12 **Listen and check.**

Developing writing skills Offering an opinion

13 **CHOICES**

A **Pick an album, a book, a series, a game and write an email (30–50 words) to a friend. Say why you liked it and why you recommend it. Use:**

- I picked …
- I like it because …
- What I like best about it …
- I recommend it to you because …

SB p. 13, 14, 15

B **Do the following tasks.**

1 **Read the task and what a student wrote. Why didn't Stevie like the last album by *Spotless*?**

Task

You've just bought the new album by *Spotless*. Write an email (40–70 words) to your friend telling him/her about it.

In your email:

- tell him/her what you think about it
- tell him/her how it compares to another album by the band
- recommend listening to it or not

From: stevie14@mailconnect.com

Subject: New album!!!

REPLY

Hi Carmen,

I'm just listening to the latest album from *Spotless*; it's called *Rescue*.

It's really awesome. I like all the tracks, but my favourite is "Hugging". The lyrics are brilliant.

I wasn't so keen on their last one – I didn't like the way it had so much piano in it, but this one is much more rock 'n' roll.

You have to listen to it.

You'll love it.

Stevie

Useful language:

- It's really awesome/ good/great …
- It's a bit disappointing …
- It's rather boring …
- My favourite band/track is …
- I'm not so keen on …
- I like / don't like the way …

2 **Now write your own answer to the following task.**

Task

You've just been to a movie. Write an email (40–70 words) to your friend telling him/her about it.

In your email:

- tell him/her the title of the movie
- tell him/her what type of movie it was
- tell him/her whether you liked it or not
- recommend watching it or not

SB p. 13

WORD FILE

Audition

- give sth **a try**
- She's got a **good voice**.
- Don't **give up!**
- He/She's going to **make it**.
- You have(n't) got **what it takes**.
- We'll **get back** to you.
- He/She's **on the way** up.

MORE Words and Phrases

1	**after**	*The police stopped the show after only 42 minutes.*	nach, nachdem
	all over	*His death was a great shock all over the world.*	überall
	attack	*She became the victim of a shark attack.*	Angriff
	benefit concert	*Elton John organised a benefit concert last year.*	Benefizkonzert
	could(n't)	*I couldn't live like that.*	könnte(n)/könntest/könntet (nicht)
	decide	*Decide what happens next.*	(sich) entscheiden
	donate	*Donate some money to support our organisation.*	spenden
	donation	*The highest donation this evening was €10,000.*	Spende
	famous	*The Rolling Stones had lots of famous songs.*	berühmt
	join	*Many people wanted to join the organisation.*	beitreten
	organise	*We have to get organised.*	organisieren, koordinieren
	raise (money)	*Let's try and raise money for the children's hospital.*	(Geld) sammeln, aufbringen
	stage	*John Lennon was on stage with his band.*	Bühne
	who	*She's the one who called you.*	der/die/das
2	be happy to	*I'm happy to help you with the shopping.*	etwas gerne tun
	cause	*We're doing this all for a good cause.*	Zweck; Grund
	celebrity	*Many celebrities showed up for the event.*	Promi, Star
	successful	*They have always been a very successful band.*	erfolgreich
	victim	*They played a concert for the victims of the accident.*	Opfer
5	**for**	*I haven't seen her for years.*	seit
	think sth of sth	*What do you think of their new single?*	etwas von etwas halten; eine Meinung zu etwas haben
6	**brave**	*You have to be brave to sing on Superstar.*	mutig, unerschrocken
	maybe	*Maybe you'll win.*	vielleicht, möglicherweise
	not even	*You don't look like a pop star. Not even like a fun version.*	(noch) nicht einmal
7	**voice**	*You have a beautiful voice.*	Stimme
8	least favourite	*My least favourite song is "Dangerously in Love".*	am wenigsten beliebt/e/er/es
G	lyrics	*The song is so fast, I can't understand the lyrics.*	Liedtext
	tune	*I like songs with a good tune.*	Melodie
ME1	Come on …	*Oh, come on, Mum!*	Jetzt hör aber auf…
	What's … like?	*What's your room like?*	Wie ist…?
ME3	**furniture**	*What furniture have you got in your room?*	Möbel
DVD	**agree**	*I'm sorry, I agree. You're not our next superstar.*	zustimmen
	awful	*I think it looks awful.*	furchtbar, schrecklich, scheußlich
	I'm sorry.	*I didn't mean to interrupt. I'm sorry.*	Das tut mir leid.
	I guess	*Yes, I guess that could be fun.*	ich nehme es an
	meet	*She met the doctors who helped her.*	begegnen
	record	*Some say their first record was the best.*	(Schall-)Platte

UNIT 2 What a coincidence!

Reading

1 Read the story. Only one title fits. Which is the right one?

☐ The lost mobile phone ☐ A lucky coincidence

☐ Camping in Scotland

The Grangers were on holiday in Scotland. They were in a small holiday house, about 60 kilometres away from Braemar.

"It's a great place for walking," Mr Granger said. But then it rained and rained for two days. Mrs Granger didn't like that. Mr Granger tried to be more positive. "A bit of rain is quite OK," he said.

The next day there was sunshine. The Grangers were happy. They drove into Braemar to do some shopping. Then they went to a café for a cup of tea. They sat at a table by the window. Suddenly, Mr Granger whispered to his wife, "Don't look. It's the Warners." Mr Warner worked with Mr Granger back home in Canterbury. Mr Granger tried to hide behind his newspaper because he didn't like Mr Warner and he didn't want to talk to him. It was too late. "I don't believe it," Bert Warner shouted, "Nick Granger! What are you doing here? On holiday? Us too. What a coincidence!"

Mr Warner came and spoke to the Grangers for ten minutes. At the end he said, "You must come and see us tomorrow! Let's have lunch together!" "What a nice idea," Mr Granger said. "No way," he said to his wife when the Warners left.

Two days later Mr Granger had an accident when he was walking through a wood. He fell over a hidden tree branch. He cut his leg really badly. His wife had to phone an ambulance. They took him to hospital. The doctor said, "You can't walk for a week."

Mr and Mrs Granger had to go home. But Mrs Granger couldn't drive. What could she do? Then she remembered the Warners. She phoned them and told them about the accident. The Warners were very happy to help. Bert picked Nick up from hospital. Then he drove the Grangers down to Canterbury. From that day on Mr Granger never said a bad word about Mr Warner.

SB p. 18, 20–24

2 How many of these tasks can you do?

1 The Granger's holiday house was in Braemar. T / F
2 The rain made Mr Granger unhappy. T / F
3 On their third afternoon in Scotland they went shopping. T / F

Complete the sentences with no more than 4 words.

4 Mr Granger didn't think Mr Warner was ....
5 Mr Granger .... Mr Warner wouldn't see him.
6 Mr Warner invited the Grangers .... the next day.

Answer the questions in one sentence.

7 What was Mr Granger doing when he hurt his leg?

....

8 How did Mr Warner help the Grangers?

....

9 What does Mr Granger think about Mr Warner now?

....

3 Check your answers.

Listening

4 How much are you like Dan? Do you think the same as him? Tick the sentences that are true for you, too. How many boxes have you ticked?

	Dan	Me	Sarah	John
1	I've got no idea what I want to be when I'm older.	☐	☐	☐
2	I'm worried about the future of our Earth.	☐	☐	☐
3	I couldn't live without loud music.	☐	☐	☐
4	The mornings are the best part of the day.	☐	☐	☐
5	I love Maths.	☐	☐	☐
6	I like to get up late at the weekends.	☐	☐	☐
7	I need more holidays.	☐	☐	☐
8	I talk too much on the phone.	☐	☐	☐
9	Money is not the most important thing in life.	☐	☐	☐
10	You never have to say sorry to a true friend.	☐	☐	☐
	total			

CD4 3

5 Listen to Sarah and John discussing the task and tick the boxes above for them. Who is most like Dan?

SB p. 18, 20–24

Essential Grammar Past continuous

6 Find seven verbs in the correct form to complete the sentences. (←→↑↓)

W	O	R	K	I	N	G	Z
A	R	E	A	D	I	N	G
T	F	P	G	P	L	A	D
C	E	E	N	L	L	R	E
H	L	I	I	I	E	E	P
I	L	A	V	E	L	A	A
N	W	O	A	Y	A	D	C
G	N	I	H	A	E	F	S
S	T	A	R	T	E	D	E

1 I was ......watching...... TV when the phone rang.

2 We were playing tennis when it .... to rain.

3 When the ball broke the window, we were .... breakfast.

4 When the lights went out, I was .... at the computer.

5 She was dancing when she .... over.

6 When the alarm clock .... , I was having a bath.

7 Bob was .... a book when there was a knock at the door.

7 Match the sentence halves.

1 At 9 a.m. I was walking ☐ the piano in the music lesson.

2 At 10 a.m. I was trying ☐ my homework.

3 At 12 a.m. I was playing ☐ Mum in the kitchen.

4 At 1 p.m. I was eating ☐ up the dishes.

5 At 2 p.m. I was talking ☐ outside the headmaster's office.

6 At 3 p.m. I was waiting ☐ not to fall asleep while my Maths teacher was talking.

7 At 5 p.m. I was helping ☐ at my desk.

8 At 6 p.m. I was washing ☐ to my friends in the French lesson (my teacher wasn't happy).

9 At 7 p.m. I was doing ☐ my lunch.

10 At 8 p.m. I was sleeping ☐ to school.

8 Complete the sentences about your day yesterday.

1 At 5 a.m. I ....

2 At 8 a.m. I ....

3 At 11 a.m. I ....

4 At 1 p.m. I ....

5 At 3 p.m. I ....

6 At 6 p.m. I ....

7 At 7 p.m. I ....

8 At 8 p.m. I ....

SB p. 25, 26

More Grammar Past continuous

9 Put the verb in brackets in the past simple or past continuous and complete the story.

I [1] was walking (walk) down the road when I [2] saw (see) a wallet on the ground. I [3] opened (open) it and [4] found (find) a £10 note in it. There was nothing else, no name, no address, no credit cards – nothing. I [5] was thinking (think) about what to do when I [6] saw (see) my friend Daisy. She [7] was shopping (shop) but she [8] didn't look (not look) very happy. I [9] asked (ask) her what was wrong. She really wanted to buy a beautiful handbag for her mum's birthday. It was £20 but she only had £10. Then I [10] knew (know) what to do with the money from the wallet.

10 Use the pictures and words to write sentences.

break leg / play football

Dawn broke her leg when she was playing football.

drink coffee / drop cup

Henry was drinking coffee when he dropped his cup

walk dog / start raining

June was walking the dog when it started raining

work at the computer / chair break

Pip was working at the computer when chair broke

read a book / headache start

Miriam was reading a book when her headache started

listen to MP3-player / crash into a lamp post

Billy was listening to his Mp3-p. when he crashed into a lamp post

fall asleep / teacher talk

Sue fell asleep when the teacher was talking

eat apple / tooth fall out

Richard tooth fell out when he eating an apple

SB p. 26

Vocabulary

11 Write numbers. Which of these objects can you:

1 listen to?
2 talk on?
3 try on?
4 pay?

12 Complete the sentences with verbs and objects from the exercise above.

1 They were so angry that they left the restaurant and they didn't ....
2 I .... but they didn't look good on me.
3 I don't think he can hear you. He's ....
4 Don't try and ask Mum anything. Can't you see she's .... with her sister.
5 I download all my music. I never ....
6 I wanted to .... but they didn't have one in my size.

13 Do the crossword and find the mystery word in 1 down.

1 to get from one side to the other of something (e.g. road, ocean, ...)
2 to want to see if a new shirt (for example) looks good on you
3 not quite the same
4 a melody
5 to make up your mind about something
6 to stay alive in a difficult situation
7 a small bag to carry things around in
8 very hard to believe
9 to go into a room, shop, etc.
10 not real, made up (e.g. a novel)
11 very big

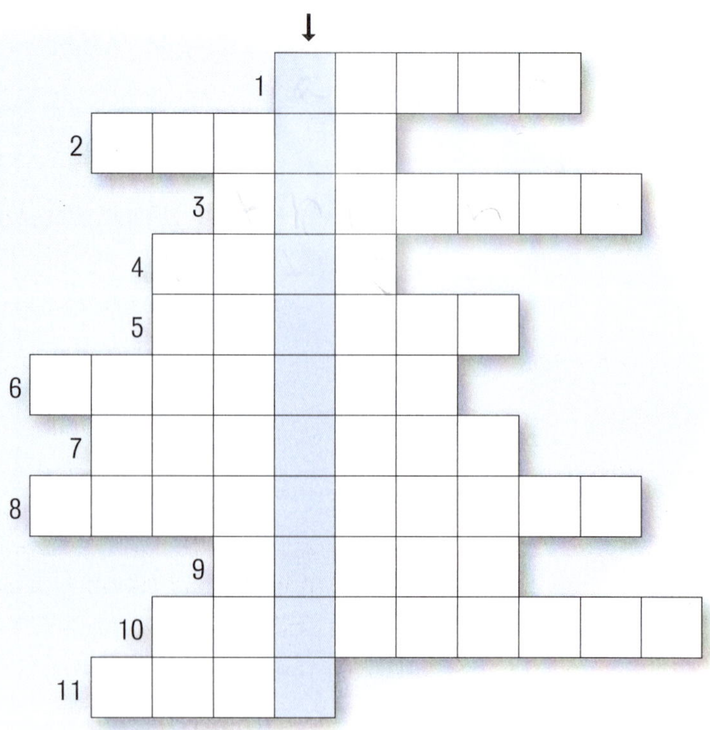

SB p. 19

14 CHOICES

A **Write a story about a coincidence (40–70 words).**

Think about:

- What was the coincidence?
- Who are the people in the story?

Start like this: A funny thing happened to me yesterday.

B **Do the following tasks.**

1 Read the task and what a student wrote. How many coincidences were there?

Task

Write a story called *Coincidence* (120–150 words).
In your story focus on:

- the people in the story
- where the story happened
- what the surprise was

Coincidence

A funny thing happened to me and my parents. They were taking me to London to see the musical *War Horse*. I think it's nice to go to London sometimes to see a nice musical. Anyway, on the train down to London the first funny thing happened. A friend of my mum and her daughter were on the train, too. They were also going to London to see *War Horse*. "What a coincidence," Mum said. "See you at the musical."

At the theatre we went to our seats. We had very nice seats. The two seats next to Mum were empty. A minute before the show started the next funny thing happened. My mum's friend and her daughter sat down right next to us. "What a coincidence," they said and we all laughed.

(133 words)

Language tip:

Using a good selection of vocabulary

When writing a text try not to use the same words all the time. Texts are better when you use a variety of words. For example, in the text the word *funny* is used three times. We could use the words *odd* and *strange* to add variety to the vocabulary.

SB p. 24

2 The words *musical* and *nice* are also used three times. Use the words in the box to replace some of these examples.

awesome	show	theatre	comfortable	popular

Writing tip:

Creating a story (1)

- When writing a story, don't start writing immediately.
- Plan the story in your head and write notes on a piece of paper.
- Think about your own life. Are there any experiences you can use for the story?
- Think about the punchline. It's the last thing your readers see. You want it to make an impression.
- Organise your paragraphs well. When there is a change in action, use a new paragraph.

3 Now write your own answer to the task in 1.

- Plan on a piece of paper.
- Think carefully about the words you use.
- Use your paragraphs well.

Everyday English The mystery boy

DVD **Look at the phrases on p. 27 in your Student's Book again. Use them to complete the dialogues.**

1 **Teacher** OK, four of you didn't do the homework. So you'll all get more homework for tomorrow.
Student .... Most of us did their homework alright, why should we do more?

2 **Sally** Hey, Gerry – .... ! There's a motorbike coming!
Gerry Phew! That was close. I didn't hear it as I had my headphones* on.

3 **Peter** It seems nobody wants me in their team.
John .... Last time we played, you never passed the ball to anybody.

4 **Lucy** I just can't concentrate when everyone is so noisy.
Anna .... I find it difficult to work here, too.

VOCABULARY: *headphones – Kopfhörer

SB p. 24, 27

MORE Words and Phrases

	coincidence	*It's a coincidence they crashed into each other's car.*	Zufall; Glück, Fügung
	incredible	*That story is incredible.*	unglaublich
	What a …!	*What a coincidence! We crashed into each other.*	Was für ein …!
1	**across**	*They travelled across the entire continent.*	über
	be about	*The film is about rabbits from Mars.*	handeln von
	called	*My mum was a huge fan of the band called The Beatles.*	hier: genannt
	few	*Only a few survived.*	wenige
	from … to …	*We travelled from New York to London.*	von … nach …
	giant	*I sat in the shade of a giant rock.*	riesig
	member	*Beyoncé began as a member of the band Destiny's Child.*	Mitglied
3	**daily**	*We bring you this programme daily.*	täglich
	fall off	*The baby fell off the balcony again.*	herunterfallen
	someone else	*Does this book belong to you or to someone else?*	jemand anders
	suitcase	*I lost my suitcase at the airport.*	Koffer
5	**bill**	*Let me pay the bill.*	Rechnung
	sunglasses	*When the sun is strong, wear sunglasses.*	Sonnenbrille
	try on	*I tried on a hat at the shop.*	anprobieren
6	I beg your pardon.	*I beg your pardon, but I'm afraid you're wrong!*	Entschuldigung, tut mir leid
	letter	*The letters DSQ went up on the board.*	Buchstabe
7a	move out (of)	*She moved out of her flat last week.*	ausziehen (aus)
	one day	*One day a shark attacks a young lady.*	eines Tages
	over there	*Can you see that car over there?*	dort drüben
	surprise	*His films have always surprised us.*	überraschen
7b	**arrive**	*Her aunt and uncle arrived a week ago.*	ankommen
	by (Ed Sheeran)	*The song "Perfect" is sung by Ed Sheeran.*	von (Ed Sheeran)
	handbag	*She has a handbag over her shoulder.*	Handtasche
	have an interest in sth	*She has a great interest in classical music.*	sich für etwas interessieren
	interrupt	*Let me finish. Please don't interrupt.*	unterbrechen
	meal	*I had my favourite meal last night. Pizza!*	Mahlzeit, Essen
	(the) movies	*Maybe we can go to the movies tomorrow.*	Kino
	not any more	*Belinda doesn't live here any more.*	nicht mehr
	pick up sth	*I picked up the money.*	etwas aufheben
	wave	*There were no waves in the morning.*	Welle
10	fall in love	*They met in Paris and fell in love.*	sich verlieben
	reach	*The album reached number one in the charts.*	erreichen
DVD	complaint	*There were complaints about the noise from neighbours.*	Beschwerde
	put up	*We put up the fence.*	aufhängen; hier: aufstellen
	surprised	*He was surprised to see her name in the book.*	überrascht
ME1	block sth	*Your bike is blocking the door.*	etwas blockieren
	leak	*There was a gas leak.*	Leck
	out there	*My mum thinks I'll get lost out there.*	da draußen
	run away	*I ran away from you because I thought you were a monster.*	weglaufen
ME2	**company**	*A man from the gas company came.*	Firma; Gesellschaft
ME4	**exam**	*Did you study for the exam?*	Test
	mark	*I got a good mark in the test.*	Note

UNIT 3 Going on a journey

Reading

1 **Read the story.**

Going to Granada

A few years ago my daughter Lucille went to Granada in Nicaragua for work. "Please come and visit me!" she said to my husband and me. So we went.

We flew to the capital Managua. It was a very long flight. Lucille met us at the airport and said, "Let's take a bus to Granada."

We went to the bus station. It didn't look like the bus stations in England. There were two old VW-buses. Two men pushed us into the first bus. We gave them some money, bought a bottle of water – and off we went.

The road was bad with holes in it. Sometimes animals like sheep or cows ran onto it. The driver went as fast as he could go. Even my husband was scared. But Lucille and the other people were having a good time.

When we got off the bus in Granada we saw lots of taxis. But Lucille said, "Let's not take a taxi. Let's take the bus to the centre." The bus was a small open van* with a wooden bench* at each side. We got in. Then some more people got in and then some more. In the end, nobody could move.

When we arrived at the hotel, I got up – and the people all moved a little for me. I don't know how, but in the end we got off the van with all our bags. The hotel was lovely – large rooms, a swimming pool and lots of beautiful trees and flowers. We loved it.

VOCABULARY: ***van** – Lieferwagen; **bench** – Sitzbank

SB p. 30, 31, 32

2 How many of these tasks can you do?

Complete the sentences with no more than 4 words.

1 The writer of the story is ....

2 Lucille's parents went to visit her in ....

3 When they got to Managua they took ....

4 At the bus station they saw that
- ☐ there weren't any buses there.
- ☐ it was very different to bus stations in the UK.
- ☐ there were lots of people there.

5 The road was bad
- ☐ but Lucille's father enjoyed the trip.
- ☐ but the driver drove really fast.
- ☐ and they often had to stop for animals.

6 The van to the centre
- ☐ was full of people.
- ☐ was much faster than a taxi.
- ☐ was very scary for Lucille.

7 Would a bus ride like the one from Managua to Granada scare you? Why (not)?

....

8 Would you take a taxi or the van in this situation? Why (not)?

....

9 You don't speak Spanish and want to get off the van. What would you do?

....

3 Check your answers.

Listening

CD4 4

4 Listen to Adrian's travel story. Find 5 mistakes in the summary. Underline them and write the correct words underneath.

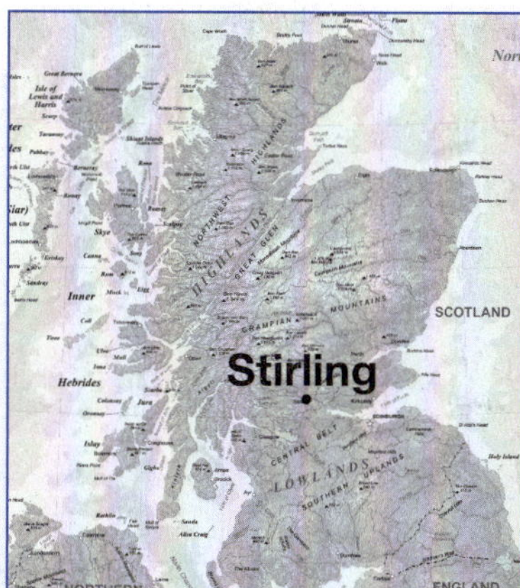

Adrian and his sister often go on holiday with their parents. Last year they were in Scotland. Adrian's dad is a big fan of Scotland. He thinks that everything there is great. During their trip they were in Stirling. Dad told them all kinds of stories about Jeremy Wallace and explained the mistakes in the book *Braveheart* to them.

It was difficult to find a place to stay for the night, but finally they found one with two rooms. In Mum and Dad's room the sofa was wet and parts of the bed were too. Dad said it was the children's fault. But Adrian saw water drops falling from the ceiling onto the bed and the carpet. They couldn't get another room, so Dad slept in the wet room and Mum slept with the kids in the other room.

In the morning Dad came to see them. He was very cold, because there was only cold water in the shower. After a quick breakfast, they had to pay for one room only. Dad was very angry about it.

1 .... 3 .... 5 ....

2 .... 4 ....

SB p. 30, 31, 32, 35

Essential Grammar Time linkers

5 Match the pictures with the sentences.

1 Before we had breakfast we watched some TV.

2 I lost my keys before I got off* the bus.

3 While we were having breakfast we were watching TV.

4 I lost my keys after I got off the bus.

5 After we had breakfast we watched some TV.

6 I lost my keys while I was getting off the bus.

VOCABULARY: *get off – aussteigen

6 Circle the right word to complete the sentences.

A terrible flight

1 *While* / *During* I was shutting my suitcase, it broke.

2 *While* / *During* the trip to the airport, we got lost.

3 There was lots of turbulence* *while* / *during* the flight.

4 *While* / *During* I was reading my book, the lights went out.

5 I dropped my cola *while* / *during* the meal and got my trousers all wet.

6 A baby was crying *while* / *during* the film and I couldn't hear anything.

7 The man in front started talking loudly *while* / *during* I was trying to get to sleep.

8 *While* / *During* I was waiting at passport control, I discovered my passport was still on the plane.

VOCABULARY: *turbulence – Turbulenz

SB p. 37

More Grammar Time linkers

7 Fill in the missing words. Use the words from the box. Sometimes there is more than one possible answer.

when by the time before while during until after

1 .... we travel to Brazil, we always watch the movie *Rio* .... we leave. We stay up .... the film is finished. .... the movie is over, my dad is always asleep.

2 .... the last day of term, my brother and I go to our grandparents' place in the country for two weeks. .... this time, we have a lot of fun riding our bikes, swimming in the lake and helping out at our grandparents' farm. My brother is lazier than me. .... I help grandpa, he sleeps in the grass behind the house.

3 We didn't go into the swimming pool .... the storm. .... we were watching the storm the lights suddenly went out. .... the lights came on again, the storm was finished.

4 .... our safari we hoped to see a tiger. We waited in our jeep .... it was dark. .... we went home, Dad wanted to walk a bit. .... the guide heard that, he only said, "Crazy man!"

More Grammar *take time to do something*

8 Write sentences. How long does it take you to ...

1 get to school? It takes me ... minutes to get to school.
2 do your homework each night? ....
3 fall asleep at night? ....
4 decide what to wear to go to a party? ....

9 Complete the text with the correct form of the verb *take*.

I love my garden.
So far it [1] .... me years to find all the plants for my garden.
Last year it [2] .... me two months to plant some rare flowers.
Now it [3] .... me half a day to water them all once a week.
A storm is coming and it [4] .... the storm ten minutes to destroy them all.

SB p. 37

Vocabulary

10 **Read Shireen's postcard and complete it with the words in the box.**

slept
suffered
hired
went
met
took
get
got

Dear Ahmed,
We're having a really great time here in Peru. It's such an amazing place and it's so good to [1] ....get.... away from London for a while. The local people are really friendly and we've [2] ....met.... some lovely people here. We spent the first week in Lima and then we [3] ....took.... a car to see a bit more of the country. We've spent some nights in hotels but we've also [4] ....slept.... in tents* too. Yesterday we [5] ....went.... up to Machu Picchu – it's fantastic. It's an ancient city high up in the Andes. Unfortunately, Mum [6] ....suffered.... from a bit of altitude sickness, so we couldn't stay too long. Guess what we saw when we came down? A snake. I [7] ....hired.... really close to it. I [8] ....got.... some really good photos. I'll show you them when we get back. Can't wait to see you.
Love,
Shireen

VOCABULARY: *tent – Zelt

11 **Match the sentence halves.**

1	hire	☐	a trip to Switzerland
2	suffer from	☐	in tents
3	go up to	☐	a car
4	sleep	☐	people
5	take	☐	to alligators
6	meet other	☐	altitude sickness
7	get too close	☐	5,000 metres

12 **Complete the sentences with the missing words.**

1 Frank .... for work at 8.00 a.m.
2 He .... his bike.
3 He .... the underground station at 8.10 a.m.
4 He .... the train at 8.15 a.m.
5 His train journey .... about 50 minutes.
6 He .... the train at around 9.05 a.m.
7 His walk to the office .... 10 minutes.
8 He .... work at 9.30 a.m.

SB p. 33

Developing speaking competencies

13 Complete the dialogue with the words in the box.

forget got that's say going correct should recommend

Sally So, Liam. I hear you're going to Brazil for your holidays. Anywhere nice?

Liam Yes, we're [1] ……going…… to Salvador in the State of Bahia.

Sally Salvador. It's a wonderful city. I was there a few years ago.

Liam Really? So what should I do there?

Sally You [2] ……should…… definitely try some of the local food. I loved it.

Liam For example?

Sally Well, you've [3] ……got…… to try Moqueca.

Liam Did you [4] ……recommend…… Moqueca?

Sally Yes, it's a fish stew. It's delicious and don't [5] ……forget…… to put some chilli sauce in it. But not too much. It's hot.

Liam OK, Moqueca with chilli sauce, is that [6] ……correct…… ?

Sally Yes, and then there's Vapata. That's also seafood. I [7] ……say…… you get that from the street sellers. It's the best.

Liam So [8] ……got…… Moqueca and Vapata. I think I should write this down before I forget.

CD4 5 **14 Listen and check.**

Developing writing skills Making a recommendation

15 CHOICES

A **You stayed at a fantastic hotel at the weekend. Write an email to a friend in which you recommend it to him/her (40–60 words).**

Use the following phrases:

- I stayed at the …
- It was great because our room …
- There was also …
- The food was … . I had … for dinner.
- There was also a pool and …

B **Do the following tasks.**

1 Read the task and what a student wrote. Why is Amy sending a link to a website?

Task **You've just come back from a holiday in a nice hotel. Write an email (40–70 words) to your friend, recommending the hotel.**

In your email:

- say where you were
- recommend it to your friend
- say what was great about the hotel

SB p. 37, 38, 39

From: amyparks@mailconnect.com

Subject: I'm back!

REPLY

Hi Tony,

We've just come back from Italy. We stayed at the Amorosa Hotel in Bettole and it was absolutely beautiful. The rooms are large and have beautiful windows, the view is excellent and it wasn't that expensive. I really recommend the hotel to you and your family. I'm sending you a link to their website because you should book soon. It's very popular.

Ciao,

Amy

Useful language:

- I (really) recommend …
- You should …
- What you should do is …
- Let me tell you that …
- I suggest …
- It's a must!
- You (really) have to …
- Try the …

2 Now write your own answer to the following task.

Task

You've just read a book you really liked. Write an email (40–70 words) to your friend recommending the book.

In your email:

- say what you read
- say what was great about the story
- recommend it to your friend

WORD FILE

Travelling

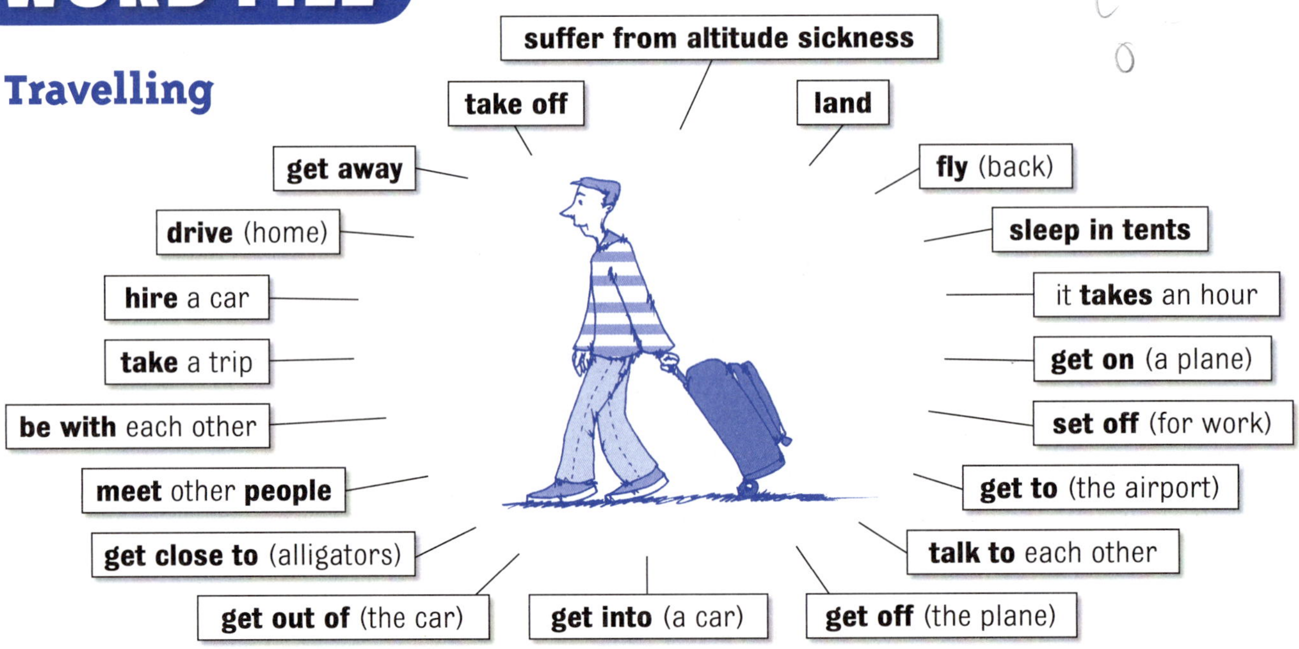

SB p. 37

MORE Words and Phrases

	traveller	*Many travellers come here by train.*	Reisende/r
1	**anyone**	*There was never anyone at the beach, so we could gallop as much as we wanted.*	irgendjemand, jede/r
	badly	*She was bleeding badly.*	sehr; hier: stark
	decision	*She made the right decision.*	Entscheidung
	end up	*She crashed her car and ended up in hospital.*	enden; landen
	explore (sth)	*They explored the land.*	erforschen, erkunden
	get out of bed	*Get out of bed now!*	aufstehen
	make sb do sth	*It made me think about the Second World War.*	jdn. dazu bringen/veranlassen etwas zu tun
	market	*I bought fresh flowers from the market.*	Markt
	on board	*On board the plane from London was Lady Gaga.*	an Bord; hier: im Flugzeug
	sail	*They wanted to sail back by sea.*	segeln
	smell	*The food on the plane had a terrible smell.*	Geruch
2	**century**	*In the 17th century, London was a much smaller city.*	Jahrhundert
	sightseeing	*Did you do any sightseeing in California?*	Besichtigung
4	explorer	*In 1804 the two explorers left their home town.*	Forscher/in
	tent	*He slept in a tent made of branches and leaves.*	Zelt
	weak	*The fire was weak but became stronger.*	schwach
5	**death**	*Lady Diana's death was a great shock.*	Tod
	foreign	*His name sounds foreign.*	ausländisch, fremd
7	**capital (city)**	*There is a nature park near Florida's capital city, Tallahassee.*	Hauptstadt
	for a while	*We want to relax for a while.*	eine Weile
	get away	*The others got away.*	davonkommen; flüchten
	look forward to sth	*We're really looking forward to the boat trip.*	sich auf etwas freuen
	prefer sth	*Which of the trips would you prefer?*	etwas vorziehen, bevorzugen
	scenery	*You can see the beautiful scenery from the mountain.*	Landschaft
9	**be afraid (of)**	*She was afraid of being alone.*	Angst haben, sich fürchten (vor)
	make friends	*I soon made friends with the people on the farm.*	sich anfreunden
11	**customer**	*Our customers are very happy with our new machine.*	Kunde/Kundin
	departure	*Check-in is two hours before departure.*	Abreise
12	**preparation**	*The producer controls the preparation of a film.*	Vorbereitung
	view	*The view of the mountains is stunning.*	Sicht; (Aus-)Blick, Aussicht
13	**at least**	*The trip was terrible, but at least I got the money back for my ticket.*	wenigstens, zumindest; mindestens
	delayed	*Our flight was delayed by an hour.*	verspätet, verzögert
	go by (sth)	*They went to New York by plane.*	hier: mit (etwas) fahren
	passport	*I forgot my passport and couldn't fly.*	Reisepass
14	**impossible**	*Who will win? It's impossible to say.*	unmöglich
15	**recently**	*Have you seen any good films recently?*	neulich, vor Kurzem
G	run out of sth	*During the trip the men ran out of food.*	etwas geht einem aus
DVD	countryside	*We really enjoyed the beautiful countryside.*	Land(schaft)
	on the way	*On the way, they stop and watch the animals.*	auf dem Weg
	recommend	*I can recommend going to the park.*	empfehlen

Reading

1 Read the text. Write the names of the animals under the pictures.

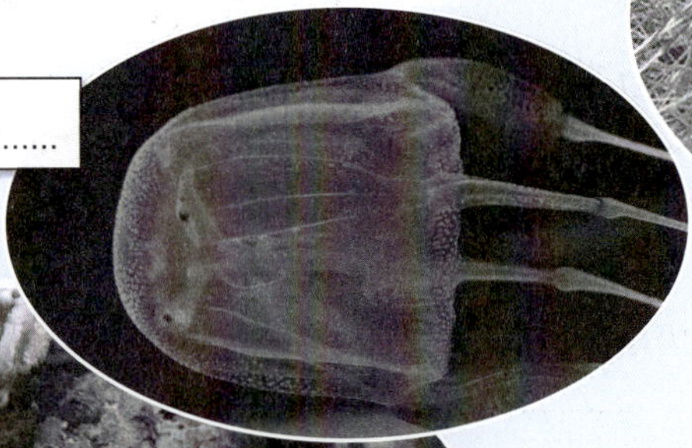

1 jellyfish

2 Snake/s

3 spider

4 Stone fish

5 crocodile

DANGEROUS CREATURES

Are you looking for dangerous animals? Then Australia is the country for you. Many of the most dangerous animals in the world live there.

The saltwater crocodile is one of the most famous dangerous animals. They are usually around 4 metres long, but sometimes they can be 7 metres! You can find them on the northeastern coast of Australia and they often hide in rivers and lakes. When you are in a boat, don't hold your arm out. A crocodile could bite it off.

Other killers are snakes and spiders. The redback spider is deadly. It lives in city areas, so you're not safe even in your own home. Snakes hide most of the time. They only attack people when they feel they are in danger. Tiger snakes are very dangerous. But if you get to a doctor quickly, you won't die from their bite.

The most dangerous animal in Australia is the jellyfish*. The box jellyfish can kill you in less than three minutes. Some people say the Irukandji jellyfish is even more dangerous because it's only 2.5 cm long and very difficult to see in the water.

But jellyfish aren't the only dangers in the sea. Watch out also for the stonefish. Its poison can kill a man in two hours.

Australia is a beautiful country. But just take care and watch out for dangerous animals when you are there. When you see a sign "Danger – crocodiles!", don't jump into the water!

VOCABULARY: ***jellyfish** – Qualle

SB p. 42, 44, 45

2 How many of these tasks can you do?

Complete the sentences with no more than 4 words.

1 The biggest saltwater crocodiles can be 2.5 cm long .
2 These crocodiles live Australia of the country.
3 On a boat tour it's a good idea not hold outside of the boat.

4 You can often find the redback spider in houses. T / F
5 Snakes are very aggressive all the time. T / F
6 A bite from the tiger snake can kill you. T / F

7 Why do some people think the Irukandji jellyfish is more dangerous than the box jellyfish?
Because it's only 2.5 cm long and very difficult to see water
8 How long do you have to get to the doctor after a stonefish bite?
Two hours
9 What advice does the writer give about the wild animals in Australia?
Sign Danger - crocodiles don't jump water

3 Check your answers.

Listening

CD4 6 **4 Listen and write *Ryan*, *Helen* or *Steve* under the correct picture. There are two extra pictures.**

white dog

corn snake
Helena

white dog
Ryan

tarantula
steve

CD4 6 **5 Listen again and answer the questions.**

1 What kind of pet does Paul think Ryan has?
Unusually snake, spider, lizard
2 How does Janet describe Ryan's dog?
small, very furry
3 What pets does Lucy guess that Helen has?
cat, dog,
4 How does Ben describe Helen's snake?
not pousinous, friendly
5 Why couldn't Steve have a dog?
too much work and bec. of his mother
6 How does Olga describe the spider?
huge hairy, agressive, ugly

Essential Grammar Comparatives and superlatives

6 Look at the information about three cars. Circle T (*True*) or F (*False*).

A

speed	160km/h
year	2013
length	3m
comfort	★★★
price	£8,000

1 Car C is more expensive than car B but not as expensive as car A. T / F
2 Car A is faster than car B but not as fast as car C. T / F
3 Car B is older than car A but not as old as car C. T / F
4 Car A is as long as car B but not as long as car C. T / F
5 Car C is more comfortable than car A and B. T / F
6 Car A is as expensive as car B. T / F
7 Car B is the longest. T / F
8 Car C is the fastest. T / F
9 Car C is as new as car B, but car A is the newest. T / F
10 Car A is the most uncomfortable. T / F

B

speed	180km/h
year	1985
length	4m
comfort	★★
price	£8,000

C

speed	200km/h
year	1967
length	3m
comfort	★
price	£25,000

7 Choose the correct adjectives to complete the text.

Sequels* are never usually as [1] *good / better* as the first film in a series. For example, *Speed* was [2] *a more awesome / an awesome* film. *Speed II* was the [3] *worse / worst* film ever made. *Spiderman* is the [4] *more exciting / most exciting* film I've seen. *Spiderman II* is [5] *boring / most boring*.

Of course, this isn't always true. What about *Shrek*, for example? I think that *Shrek II* is [6] *good / better* than *Shrek*. I think that it is [7] *funnier / funniest* and I also think the story is [8] *more interesting / most interesting*. Don't get me wrong. I like *Shrek*, it's a [9] *great / greatest* film. It's [10] *more / most* intelligent than most Hollywood films. But I just don't think it is as [11] *funny / funnier* as the second part. I think *Shrek II* is the [12] *greater / greatest* cartoon ever made.

VOCABULARY: *sequel – Folge, Fortsetzung

SB p. 43, 48

More Grammar Comparatives and superlatives

8 Complete the sentences with a superlative.

1 A Charles and George are good at Maths.
B Yeah but I'm the best.

2 A Tammy and Georgina have got really cute dogs.
B Yeah, but my dog is the cutest ✓

3 A Nigel's and Geoff's girlfriends are really pretty.
B Yeah, but my girlfriend is the prettiest ✓

4 A Paul and Steve have got really cool bikes.
B Yeah, but my bike is the coolest ✓

5 A The teacher said that the twins are really intelligent.
B Yeah, but I'm the most ~~intelligentest~~ intelligent ✓

6 A My mum and dad have got really expensive cars.
B Yeah, but my dad's car is the most expensive ✓

9 In your exercise book, rewrite the sentences so that they mean the same.

Example: Anna is older than Janet. → Janet is not as old as Anna.

1 Squash is more exciting than tennis.
2 Rome is bigger than Naples.
3 Finland is not as hot as Greece.
4 Hungarian is not as easy as Spanish.
5 Natasha is much friendlier than Victoria.
6 The hotel in Edinburgh was much worse than the hotel in Glasgow.
7 Romantic films are not nearly as exciting as fantasy films.
8 Detective films are not nearly as funny as cartoons.

10 What do you think of these paintings? Write sentences to compare them. Use the adjectives in the box to help you.

A

B

C

~~old~~
beautiful
good
~~modern~~
exciting
~~interesting~~
~~ugly~~

Painting A is the oldest.
I think painting B is the most beautiful.
Painting A is more interesting than the others.
The B painting is ugly.
Picture C is more modern.
Painting A is better.
Picture B is more exciting.

SB p. 48

Vocabulary

11 Find nine adjectives in the word snake. Then write them down.

elegantaggressivedangerouspoisonouscuddlyfurrystunningdeadlycute

1 elegent
2 aggressive
3 dangerous
4 poisonous
5 cuddly
6 furry
7 ...
8 ...
9 ...

12 Choose the correct adjective.

1 That snake is *deadly / furry / stunning*. One bite and it kills you.
2 Her dog is so *aggressive / cuddly / elegant*. I just want to hold it in my arms.
3 His rabbit's got a lot of hair. It's very *stunning / furry / dangerous*.
4 That bird is bright red, yellow and blue. It's absolutely *stunning / deadly / cute*.
5 Don't drink that! It's *cuddly / aggressive / poisonous*.
6 It's a very *dangerous / stunning / poisonous* part of town. We never go there at night.
7 Don't touch that dog. It's very *furry / stunning / aggressive* and might attack you.
8 Dave wore his best clothes to the party, a beautiful suit and tie. He looked very *furry / elegant / poisonous*.

13 Unscramble the words to complete the dialogue.

Helena Look at that animal. It's [1] ~~ared~~ adorble (arodlbea). What is it?
Juliet It's a slow loris. It looks cute, but it's quick to [2] .... (tkatac).
Helena Really? Why?
Juliet To [3] .... (feeddn) its young. It produces a [4] .... (oopsin) that can be deadly.
Helena That sounds pretty [5] .... (thgirnnfgei). I [6] .... (popsuse) I better [7] .... (tyas) away from it then.
Juliet Good idea, I totally [8] .... (regae).

SB p. 43

14 CHOICES

A **Write a fact file about your favourite animal (40–70 words).**

In your fact file say:

- what animal it is
- how big/long/heavy it is
- what it looks like
- why it is your favourite animal

B **Do the following tasks.**

1 Read the task and what a student wrote. Why do we need sharks?

Task **Write a fact file about an endangered animal (120–170 words).**
In your fact file, say:

- what the animal is and what it looks like
- why it is endangered
- why it is important to you to save it
- where it can be found
- what we could do to save it

The endangered animal I want to write about is the mako shark. Here's what you need to know.

- There are two types, shortfin and longfin.
- They are big (3.2 to 4.5 metres).
- They can weigh up to 800 kgs.
- They hardly ever attack humans.

Mako sharks are found in all warm oceans. They live in the seas off Asia, Brazil and in the Gulf Stream, but there have also been mako shark sightings around France and Italy. They are endangered because fishing boats (especially in Asia) hunt them.

· because their meat is great
o because their fins* are used for medicine

Some fishing fleets only take the fins and throw the fish back to die. This is terrible. That is why we should forbid the fishing of mako sharks. And we shouldn't buy their meat.

I think that sharks are important because

› they eat older and dying fish
✦ they keep the ocean clean from other dangerous fish

Save the mako shark!!!!!!!!!!!!!

VOCABULARY: *fin – Flosse

Language tip:

Using good punctuation

When writing a text, be consistent (einheitlich). For example when you are doing bullet points, use one type of bullet point only and lay them out clearly. But only use them when you have several points to make.

For strong messages use exclamation marks (!) but don't overdo them. And never use more than one exclamation mark in a row!

2 Look at the text again.

1 What is wrong with the bullet points?
2 Should you use them in all of the examples above? Why (not)?
3 Where else could you put exclamation marks? Mark them in.
4 Where in the text is the writer using too many exclamation marks?

Writing tip:

Writing a fact file

- Carefully check your facts.
- If you use the internet, don't only look at one site. Check the information on several.
- Do not copy the text but rephrase using your own words.
- Do not copy over difficult words you do not understand.
- Lay your page out well. Use one or two pictures to help the reader understand your text.

3 Now write your own answer to the following task.

Task

Write a fact file about your favourite animal (120–170 words).
In your fact file, say:

- what the animal is and what it looks like
- where it can be found
- what its life is like
- why it is your favourite animal
- why it is important to you

Everyday English Dangerous dogs

DVD **Look at the phrases on p. 49 in your Student's Book again. Use them to complete the dialogues.**

1 A Did you hear Jenny playing the guitar? I think she's terrible.
B I don't agree. .... – she's not a good player, but she's not terrible!

2 A Do you think we should get a dog for grandma?
B Well, ... It'd be great for her to have a pet for company, but maybe a dog would be too much work for her.

3 A Do you think Mrs Morrison would look after Blackie while we're away?
B .... She said no last time we asked her.
A Yeah, ... Maybe we need to ask somebody else.

SB p. 48, 49

MORE Words and Phrases

1	(not) at all	*You're not bothering me at all!*	überhaupt nicht
	cute	*Shrek is too cute for me.*	niedlich, süß
	deadly	*The bite of the taipan snake is deadly.*	tödlich
	probably	*There are some fascinating things about sharks that you probably don't know yet.*	wahrscheinlich, vermutlich
	rabies	*Rabies is a very dangerous illness in animals.*	Tollwut
	seal	*Seals and sea lions are the great white shark's food.*	Seehund, Robbe
6	bleed	*He fell over and his knee started bleeding.*	bluten
	bleeding	*He helped control the bleeding.*	Blutung
	calm	*In a loud but calm voice she said what happened.*	ruhig, gelassen
	contact sb	*An organisation contacted her.*	sich mit jdm in Verbindung setzen
	event	*Her first concert in the US was an important event.*	Ereignis
	heart	*Bethany's heart beats faster every time she sees something dark in the water.*	Herz
	neither	*She tried one wave, but it didn't work. Neither did the next or next.*	auch nicht; weder; keine
	nightmare	*A dream can turn into a nightmare.*	Albtraum
	offer	*They offered her a job as a photographer.*	anbieten
	offer	*It was an interesting offer.*	Angebot
	panic	*She didn't panic after the shark attacked her.*	in Panik geraten
	several	*Meryl Streep starred in several films.*	einige; verschiedene
	wrap sth	*He wrapped his shirt around Bethany's wound.*	etwas einwickeln
7	**fear**	*Her dreams are bigger than her fear.*	Angst
	need to	*I need to study for the test.*	müssen
	scream	*At the airport there were a lot of screaming fans.*	schreien
11	**e.g.**	*You can eat tropical fruit there, e.g. mango, pineapple and papaya.*	z.B.
	expensive	*That shirt is too expensive!*	teuer
	horrible	*I think this movie is just horrible!*	grausam, furchtbar
12	**advise sb against sth**	*Gillian advises against swimming with sharks.*	jdm von etwas abraten, jdn vor etwas warnen
	defend	*Sharks kill to defend their territory.*	verteidigen
	diver	*Swimmers and people snorkelling are in more danger than divers.*	Taucher/in
	explain	*Our teacher explained the problem.*	erklären; erläutern
	feed	*After a large meal, crocodiles don't need to feed for a long time.*	fressen
	frightening	*A shark's mouth is a frightening sight.*	erschreckend, beängstigend
	great white shark	*You can sometimes see great white sharks jumping out of the water.*	Weißer Hai
	however	*There aren't many species of shark that attack humans. However, some can be very dangerous.*	aber; dennoch; allerdings
	length	*Sharks can grow up to the length of two cars.*	Länge
	mistake sth for sth	*Sharks sometimes mistake humans for seals.*	etwas mit etwas verwechseln
	not so much	*But not so much here in California.*	nicht wirklich
	on average	*Great whites kill only one person every 8 years on average.*	im Durchschnitt
	suppose	*I suppose it does. But not here in California.*	annehmen
	take care	*People should take care.*	aufpassen, sich hüten
13	**search**	*Search the internet for more information.*	durch-, absuchen
ME1	accent	*Has he got an accent?*	Akzent
	fair	*He's got fair hair.*	blond, hell
DVD	**be (not) allowed to do sth**	*I wasn't allowed to ride the London Eye.*	etwas (nicht) tun dürfen

UNIT 5 London calling!

Reading

1 **Read Susan's letter.**

Dear Aunt Helen,

I've just got back from a school trip to London. We were there for three days. I'm really tired now. We walked for hours every day – but it was cool.

We saw all the famous places, so that made my mum happy too. I liked St Paul's Cathedral best. We walked up all the 500+ steps. From the top we had a great view of London. The view from the London Eye the next day wasn't so good. It was quite foggy and we couldn't see much. We also saw a film in a big cinema in Leicester Square – the cinema is fantastic but the tickets were very expensive.

On our first evening we went to the Globe Theatre and saw a Shakespeare play. It was called *A Comedy of Errors*. OK, the language was a little strange, but I had no problems understanding it. We laughed quite a lot. The only thing I hated was that we had to stand for two hours. We had cheap tickets so we didn't get a seat!

The best thing of all was the shopping, of course! The teachers gave us two hours of free time every day. Lucy and I went to Camden Market. She bought a funny hat there – it's red with a big white flower in it! She thought it was really cool. I wasn't so sure. So I didn't buy one for me.

Yesterday was our last day and we went to the Science Museum. Now, that really is a great museum. There are lots of working machines with lots of buttons to press.

Hope to see you soon.
Love,
Susan

SB p. 52, 53

2 How many of these tasks can you do?

1 Susan is tired after the trip because
- ☐ they had to go everywhere on foot.
- ☐ they didn't sleep much.
- ☐ they arrived home late.

2 Susan's mum said she should
☐ buy her a present. ☐ enjoy the sights of London. ☐ not spend too much money.

3 Susan thought St Paul's Cathedral
☐ had too many steps. ☐ was higher than the London Eye. ☐ was really good.

4 Susan found *A Comedy of Errors* difficult to understand. T / F
5 Susan and her friends thought the comedy was very funny. T / F
6 The play was nearly three hours long. T / F

Answer the questions in one sentence.

7 How many hours in total did Susan spend shopping?

....

8 What did Susan think of what Lucy bought?

....

9 What did Susan like about the Science Museum?

....

3 Check your answers.

Listening

CD4 7

4 First, read about Dick Whittington. Then listen to the conversation about him. Are the sentences (1–8) fact or fiction? Circle the correct option.

Most of us have heard the story of Dick Whittington, the poor man who became extremely rich and then became the mayor* of London. And most of us probably think the story is a legend – a bit like Robin Hood. But in fact he was a real person. However, the story we heard when we were children is not completely true.

1 He came from a poor family. *fact / fiction*
2 He was mayor of London four times. *fact / fiction*
3 He had a cat. *fact / fiction*
4 He made a lot of money selling his cat. *fact / fiction*
5 After hearing some church bells* he decided to return to London. *fact / fiction*
6 He made money from the King's family. *fact / fiction*
7 He knew kings. *fact / fiction*
8 He gave a lot of money to the poor. *fact / fiction*

VOCABULARY
***find one's fortune** – sein Glück finden
mayor – Bürgermeister/in
church bells – Kirchenglocken

SB p. 52, 53

Essential Grammar Relative pronouns

5 Underline the relative pronouns in the quiz. Then do the quiz.

1 What's the name of the river which flows* through London?
a) ☐ the Severn c) ☐ the Thames
b) ☐ the Dee

2 Many tourists who go to London want to see Big Ben. But what is Big Ben?
a) ☐ a clock c) ☐ a bell
b) ☐ a tower

3 What is the name of the giant wheel which is on the south bank of the river?

a) ☐ the London Eye
b) ☐ the London Wheel
c) ☐ the London Roundabout

4 What's the name of the architect who designed St Paul's Cathedral?
a) ☐ Charles Dickens
b) ☐ Christopher Wren
c) ☐ Tim Vickery

5 What do you call the guards who protect the Crown Jewels?
a) ☐ Steakmen c) ☐ Beefeaters
b) ☐ Porklovers

6 Who was the famous writer who kept a diary of London life in the 1600s?
a) ☐ Samuel Pepys
b) ☐ Christopher Wren
c) ☐ William Shakespeare

7 What's the name of the area of London which was a flower market until about 40 years ago?
a) ☐ Covent Garden c) ☐ Hyde Park
b) ☐ Waterloo

8 What is the name of the famous fictional detective whose address is 221B Baker Street?
a) ☐ James Bond c) ☐ Alex Rider
b) ☐ Sherlock Holmes

9 What is the name of the London football team whose stadium is called Stamford Bridge?
a) ☐ Arsenal c) ☐ Chelsea
b) ☐ West Ham

VOCABULARY: *flow – fließen

6 Choose the correct word to complete the sentences.

1 La Trattoria is the restaurant *who / whose / which* makes the best pizza in town.
2 Gareth Bale is the footballer *who / whose / which* Real Madrid paid a lot of money for.
3 Janet is the girl *who / whose / which* sits next to me in French.
4 He's the man *who / whose / which* dog wakes me up every morning at 6 a.m.
5 Manchester is the city *who / whose / which* has the best football teams in the UK.
6 They're the people *who / whose / which* daughter is an opera singer.
7 Miriam is the girl *who / whose / which* birthday is on the same day as yours.
8 Euston is the station *who / whose / which* is the busiest in London.
9 Mr Thomas is the teacher *who / whose / which* teaches us English.

7 In which of the sentences in 6 is *that* also possible. Tick the boxes.

1 ☐ 2 ☐ 3 ☐ 4 ☐ 5 ☐ 6 ☐ 7 ☐ 8 ☐ 9 ☐

SB p. 54, 55, 58

More Grammar Relative pronouns

8 **Put the words in order to make sentences.**

1 man / made the film / *Jurassic Park* / the / who / is / Spielberg

Spielberg is the man who made the film *Jurassic Park*.

2 the girl / know / lives upstairs? / Do / that / you

Do you know that the girl lives upstairs?

3 to / this / goes / which / Piccadilly Circus? / Is / the bus

Is this the bus which goes to Piccadilly Circus

4 I've got / London. / lives / who / a / in / friend

I've got a friend who lives in London

5 you / you / much? / liked / T-shirt / which / Did / the / so / buy

~~Did you liked the T-shirt~~

6 the / Where's / this door? / who / key / the / has / to / woman

9 **Complete the sentences with your own ideas.**

1 Mum is the person in our house who ....

2 My bedroom is the place that ....

3 The headmaster is the person whose ....

4 My best friend is the person who ....

5 Reading is a hobby that ....

6 Parents are the people whose ....

10 **Write sentences like in the example in your exercise book. Use your own ideas.**

Example: William Shakespeare is the man who wrote *Romeo and Juliet*.

SB p. 58

Vocabulary

11 Write the words under the pictures.

square tower park shopping centre art gallery
street bridge museum shops buildings

1 bridge

2 art gallery

3 buildings

4 tower

5 shops

6 shopping centre

7 park

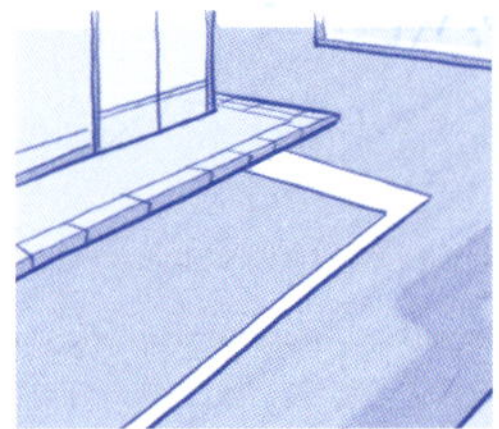

8 street

9 square

10 museum

12 Use the clues to complete the crossword and find the secret word.

(Clue: It's the name of one of London's railway stations.)

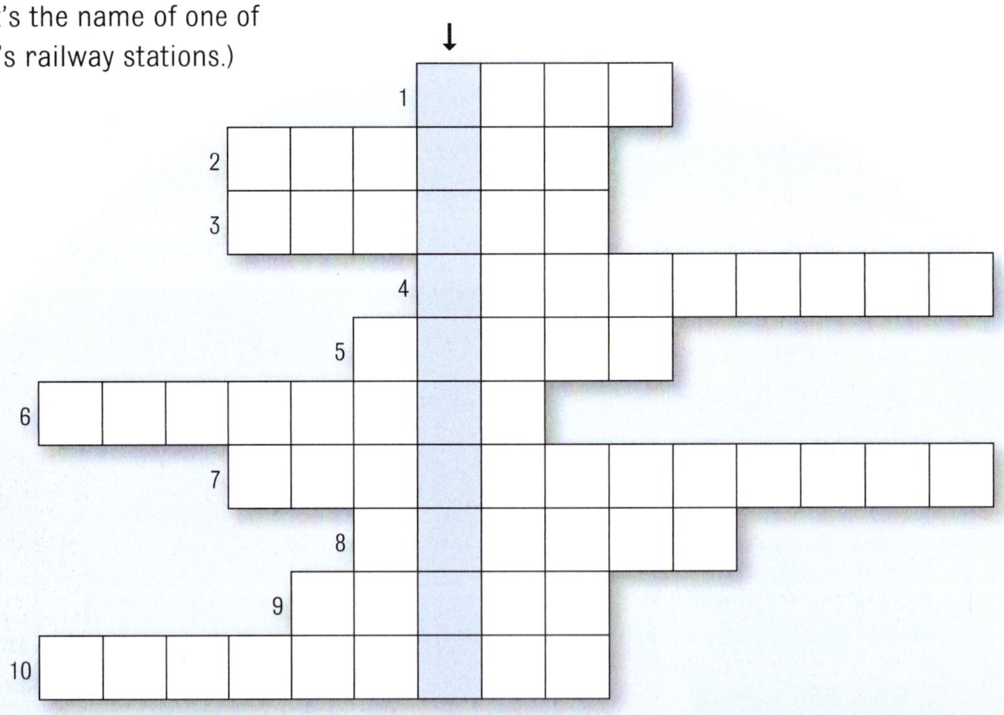

1 Relax and watch the world go by in Hyde …
2 Take a photo of Nelson and his lions in Trafalgar …
3 Watch boats sail under Tower …
4 Visit Soho, one of London's most famous …
5 Take a boat trip on the … Thames.
6 Take a train ride from one of London's many …
7 Visit Tate. One of the best … in the world.
8 Walk down Oxford … and look in the shops.
9 Covent Garden has cool …
10 Go and look at some of London's modern … like City Hall and The Shard.

SB p. 54, 55, 56, 57

13 CHOICES

A **You were on a short holiday. Write an email (40–70 words) to a friend and tell him/her about it.**

In your email say:

- where you were
- who was with you
- what you liked best and why

B **Do the following tasks.**

1 Read the task and what a student wrote. What is Hanna really interested in?

Task **Imagine you are on a holiday in Oxford. Write an email or letter to your uncle (120–180 words).**

Write about:

- where you're staying
- what you've bought
- some of the sights
- the things you like best
- your plans for tomorrow

Dear Uncle Lawrence,

Finally! We've made it to Oxford for the weekend, and Mum and Dad are visiting old friends, so I've got some time for myself. We're staying at a bed & breakfast in Abdingdon Road. Its only a 20-minute walk to the city centre, so thats OK. This morning Mum and Dad dragged me to the Ashmolean Museum, but after that I went to Christ Church College on my own to see the Harry Potter dining hall there. Awesome! I took some really great photo's. There are some great places in Oxford, but Christ Church with it's hall is the best.

I also went to that large bookshop you told me about. I didn't buy a book, but they had a magic wand like Harry uses so I bought that. Thank you for the money you gave me, it was a big help.

Tomorrow it's going to rain so I cant go punting on the river. I hope the day wont be boring. Maybe I'll go to the cinema. There's an afternoon show of "Fantastic Beasts 2".

Best wishes,
Hanna

Language tip:

Apostrophes

Apostrophes can be difficult to get right. Sometimes students add them when they are not needed (No Dog's Allowed), other times they miss them out altogether (Carolines letter).

SB p. 58

2 Look at the text again. Look at the highlighted words and correct the ones that are wrong.

Writing tip:

Writing an email / a letter to a friend, a relative* …

Consider the following for your writing:

- Who are you writing to?
- Are there any questions from their letter you have to answer?
- Do you want to say thank you for anything?
- Do you have questions yourself?
- What do you want to tell them? What is your news?
- Don't forget to ask how the other person is.
- End your letter with *Best wishes*, *Love*, *Yours*, etc.

VOCABULARY
***relative** – Verwandte/r

3 Now write your own answer to the following task.

Task

Imagine you are on holiday somewhere in Austria. Write an email or letter to a relative (120–180 words).

Write about:

- where you're staying
- what you're doing
- people you have met
- the things you like best
- food and weather
- your plans for tomorrow

Everyday English The raffle ticket

DVD **Look at the phrases on p. 59 in your Student's Book again. Use them to complete the dialogues.**

1 A You want to buy yourself a new bike? Then why don't you make some money by washing people's cars?

B ………………………………………… . But I'm not sure there are many people who want their car washed.

A Maybe not. But ………………………………………… , isn't it?

2 A Mum? Can I go to Greece on a camping tour with my friends during the holidays?

B ………………………………………… , Nick! You're only fourteen! Of course you can't go!

3 A Look, Ruby, help me tidy up the house and I'll take you to your favourite restaurant on Sunday.

B OK, Dad, but only if I can have a double portion of lemon ice cream!

A ………………………………………… !

SB p. 58, 59

WORD FILE

Around town

a **street**	a **building**	a **tower**	an **art gallery**	a **river**
a **square**	a **bridge**	a **museum**	a **park**	a **shop / shopping centre**

MORE Words and Phrases

	sights	*We looked at all the sights in Los Angeles.*	Sehenswürdigkeiten
1	**attraction**	*Take a look at the many attractions London offers.*	Sehenswürdigkeit
	avoid	*You should avoid going there at noon – there are too many people.*	vermeiden
	building	*Look at that beautiful old building over there.*	Gebäude
	collection	*Tate Modern has a great collection of art.*	Sammlung
	gallery	*The old factory building is now an art gallery.*	Galerie
	giant wheel	*The London Eye is a giant wheel.*	Riesenrad
	government	*The British government meets in the Houses of Parliament.*	Regierung
	hand	*The giant clock's hands are 2.7 and 4.3 metres long.*	Zeiger (Uhr)
	the Houses of Parliament	*When you go to London, you must see the Houses of Parliament.*	das Parlament (von Großbritannien)
	in advance	*Book your ride in advance.*	im Voraus
	including	*Entry to all the buildings here including the museum is free today.*	einschließlich
	play	*We watched a play by Shakespeare in London.*	Theaterstück
	queue	*There's always a long queue at the Tower of London.*	Schlange, Reihe
	raise	*They raise the bridge to let ships go through.*	(an-)heben, hochziehen
	raven	*Make sure to look for the ravens at the Tower of London.*	Kolkrabe
	theatre	*Shakespeare played in the Globe Theatre.*	Theater
	visitor	*Visitors can go in City Hall.*	Besucher/in
	which	*This is the shop which sells the best cakes.*	welche/r/s
5	**against**	*Some kids are against the idea.*	gegen
	entertainment	*Go to Covent Garden and watch the street entertainment.*	Unterhaltung
	exercise	*I should get more exercise.*	hier: Bewegung
	exist	*Torture still exists in some countries.*	existieren
	memorial	*The memorial to Princess Diana is in Hyde Park.*	Denkmal
	right(s)	*Stand up for your rights!*	Recht(e)
	torture	*The London Dungeon was a prison famous for torture and death.*	Folter
	traffic	*There's a lot of traffic in London.*	Verkehr
	underground	*This underground museum is about torture.*	unterirdisch
7a	loads of (informal)	*You can go to loads of concerts in London.*	eine Menge
	skin	*There are many people with different colours of skin in London.*	Haut
9	thrilling	*A ride on the London Eye can be thrilling.*	aufregend
ME1	figure out	*I can figure this out.*	herausfinden; ausrechnen; verstehen
	right	*It's right over there!*	genau; gleich
	(shopping) arcade	*Where is the shopping arcade?*	(Einkaufs-)Passage

UNIT 6 What will happen if ...?

Reading

1 **Read the story.**

The Maths test

It was the day before the Maths test! I don't like Maths. I just don't understand it. I hate numbers. Give me words. I love words.

I was looking at my Maths book. But I just didn't understand it. I kept thinking about my birthday on Friday. If I get a bad mark* in my Maths test, there won't be a party. I was sad.

Then I remembered. It was my birthday. I could make a wish. So I made my wish three days before my birthday. I wished for the best birthday party ever.

Then I made a second wish, "Please, please let me get the best mark in the class." Then I went to bed. I was tired from all the wishing.

The next day was test day. I put a photo of Raffles on the desk. He's my dog and it's my lucky charm*. The test was very difficult. I didn't have a good feeling about it. "Maybe, just maybe, it's not as bad as I fear," I said to myself.

The next day I got to school and I was really nervous. Results. Was this the end of my party? We got to the classroom, but my Maths teacher was not there. She was ill. I was happy.

"That's good," I thought. "I can have a great party!" Maybe the second wish will come true too?

It was the best party ever. And the second wish? Well, on Monday morning I got my results. 33.33% exactly. The worst result in the class. Not great.

There will be another party next year. And there will be another test. Maybe I'll start studying right away. Or tomorrow. Yes, I'll really start tomorrow.

VOCABULARY: ***mark** – Note; **lucky charm** – Glücksbringer

SB p. 62–66

2 How many of these tasks can you do?

Complete the sentences with no more than 4 words.

1 Cathy doesn't .... , but she loves words.

2 Instead of studying for Maths she was thinking ....

3 If she wants a party, Cathy has to get a ....

4 The day before the test, Cathy

- ☐ made two wishes.
- ☐ made a wish to understand all the Maths problems.
- ☐ started studying hard for the test.

5 Cathy's lucky charm

- ☐ was on her desk at home.
- ☐ is a picture of her dog.
- ☐ always worked.

6 The test was difficult

- ☐ and Cathy hoped for another chance in a new test.
- ☐ but Cathy hoped it wasn't as bad as she feared.
- ☐ and Cathy knew right away there was no birthday party this year!

7 Why did Cathy have a birthday party after all?

....

8 How does Cathy describe the party?

....

9 How did Cathy do in the test?

....

3 Check your answers.

Listening

CD4 8

4 Listen to Akira (Japan), Carmita (Mexico) and Luis (Spain) talking about superstitions in their countries. Then circle T (*True*) or F (*False*).

1 In Japan people are quite superstitious. T / F

2 Japanese people consider white snakes to be a good thing. T / F

3 There are a lot of white snakes in Japan. T / F

4 In Mexico, you have to pray* to San Antonio for 10 nights. Then he will help you. T / F

5 Carmita is going to buy a statue of San Antonio. T / F

6 Carmita is sure she'll find a boyfriend without San Antonio. T / F

7 A lot of students live in Salamanca. T / F

8 The frog on the door of the university is made of stone. T / F

9 Students touch the frog with both hands for good luck. T / F

VOCABULARY: *pray – beten

SB p. 62-66, 67

Essential Grammar 1st Conditional

5 Read the sentences and tick the correct picture.

1 If you wear that shirt, you'll look really good.

2 If you invite her to the cinema, I'm sure she'll say yes.

3 If you touch that dog, it won't bite you.

4 If it's hot tomorrow, we'll go to the beach.

5 If you phone me at nine, I won't be home.

6 If we leave now, we'll be home by ten.

6 Underline the correct forms.

1 **A** Come on. Hurry up.
B Don't worry. If we *miss* / *will miss* the bus, we *take* / *will take* a taxi.

2 **A** I don't want to eat an orange, Mum.
B But if you *don't eat* / *won't eat* fruit, you *get* / *will get* a cold.

3 **A** I'm sorry. I'm really busy.
B Oh please! If you *help* / *will help* me, I *give* / *will give* you my best pen.

4 **A** Jeff eats too many sweets.
B I know. If he *doesn't stop* / *won't stop* eating sweets, he *has* / *will have* problems with his teeth.

5 **A** Oh no! I'm going to be late for school again.
B No, you're not. You *are* / *will be* OK if you *run* / *will run*.

6 **A** She *goes* / *will go* to the party if you *invite* / *will invite* her.
B Do you think so? I don't think she likes me very much.

SB p. 68, 69

More Grammar 1st Conditional

7 Use the words to make questions.

1 What / you do / rain / at the weekend? What will you do if it rains at the weekend?

2 What programme / you watch / turn on the TV tonight?
What programme will you watch if you turn on the TV tonight.

3 What / you eat / feel hungry / after dinner tonight?
What will you eat if you feel hungry after dinner tonight.

4 Where / you go / go away / this weekend?
Where will you go if you go away this weekend

5 What / you play / play sport / this weekend?
What will you play if you play sport this weekend

6 Who / you talk to / phone someone / tonight?
Who will you talk to if you phone someone tonight

8 Look at the picture. Write down what Lucas says.

1 If my dad is angry with me, he doesn't speak to me for a week.

2 If my mother is angry with me, she doesn't take me to school when it rains.

3 If my grandfather is angry with me, he doesn't give me money.

4 If my sister is angry with me, she doesn't let me play computer games.

5 If my friend is angry with me, he doesn't play football with me.

6 If my dog is angry with me, he doesn't go out with me.

9 Rewrite the sentences using *unless*. Use your exercise book.

1 I won't help him with his work if he doesn't ask me to.
I won't help him with his work unless he asks me to.

2 If it is not very important, he won't phone me. He won't phone me ... its not important

3 He will be sick if he doesn't stop eating. He won't be sick unless he stops eating

4 If you don't study for the test, there won't be a party. There ... party unless

5 You will be late if you don't run. You will be late unless you run

6 Mary won't have to go there if she doesn't want to. Mary will have to go unless she doesn't want to

7 He won't speak if you don't speak to him first. He won't speak unless you don't speak to him first

SB p. 69

Vocabulary

10 Complete the mini-dialogues with the sentences from the box.

Because it'll bring me bad luck, of course.	I just don't. I think we make our own luck.
No, not at all.	Yes, I am. Very.
No, I don't. I think they're silly.	Well, for example, I never walk under a ladder.

1 **A** Are you superstitious?
B Yes, I am. Very.
A What sort of things do you do?
B Well for example, I never walk under a ladder.
A Why not?
B Because it'll bring me bad luck, of course.

2 **A** Do you believe in superstitions?
B No, I don't. I think they're silly.
A Why not?
B I just don't. I think we make our own luck.
A So you don't have a lucky charm, for example?
B No, not at all.

11 Complete with the correct forms of *bring, make, come*.

If you break a mirror
It [1] bring bad luck they say
And if you break a vase
Would that be OK?
If you see a rainbow,
[2] Will Make a wish? Yes or no?
Will the wish [3] come true
I don't think so; well, do you?
I [4] made so many wishes
None [5] came ever true
Maybe [6] making many wishes
[7] bring bad luck to you.

12 Match the words with the pictures.

- [3] pavement
- [4] ladder
- [5] campfire
- [2] tiger's eye
- [1] mirror

1 
2 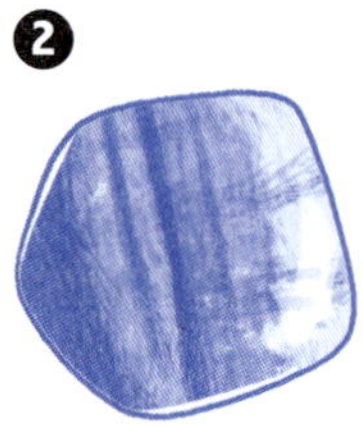
3 
4 
5 

SB p. 66, 68, 69

Developing speaking competencies

13 Put the dialogue in the correct order.

☐	**Connor**	There's a new roller disco opening. Do you want to go?
☐	**Connor**	It's at the sport centre.
☐	**Connor**	Are you free on Friday evening?
☐	**Connor**	That'd be great. I won't be late.
☐	**Connor**	Roller disco and pizza. Sounds like the perfect evening.
☐	**Connor**	Around half past seven, eight o'clock.
☐	**Dawn**	Neither will I. And after we could go to the pizza restaurant. How about it?
☐	**Dawn**	I'd love to. Where is it?
☐	**Dawn**	Eight, that should be OK. Why?
☐	**Dawn**	Let me see. What time?
☐	**Dawn**	OK, why don't we meet outside at about 7.45?

CD4 9

14 Listen and check.

Developing writing skills Making arrangements

15 CHOICES

A Write a note to your parents (40–70 words) and tell them about your plans for the afternoon.

Say:

- where you are going
- who is with you
- when you'll be back
- what you'd like for dinner

Start like this: Hi Mum and Dad. It's 3 p.m. and I'm ...

B Do the following tasks.

1 Read the task and what a student wrote. What should Mum do if there is a problem?

Task

You've just found a note on the refrigerator door. It says:

Had to leave early. What about the arrangements for the evening? Let me know and be back by 6. Love, Mum

You write a note (40–70 words) back in which you say:

- what your plans are
- what Mum should do
- what you suggest

SB p. 69, 70, 71

Dear Mum,
Can't be back by 6. I suggest we meet at the train station.
I'll phone Kate to let her know we'll get to her place around nine. Let's just take a taxi.
And what about bringing her that cake in the fridge as a surprise?
See you at the station.
If there's a problem, phone me in the afternoon.
Love,
Amy

Useful phrases:

Making arrangements

- Let's meet / go to / do …
- Why don't you … ?
- Why can't you … ?
- I suggest …
- What about meeting … ?

2 Now write your own answer to the following task.

Task

You've just found a note on the refrigerator door. It says:

Tim, you sleepyhead. What about football training in the afternoon? Leave me a note, phone's dead. Bye, Ken

You write a note (40–70 words) back in which you tell Ken:

- when the football training is
- that he should take your bag with him
- where to meet to go to football training together

WORD FILE

Luck

a wish **comes true**

make a wish

wish for (money)

pick up (some money)

have (good/bad) **luck**

bring (good/bad) **luck**

get (good/bad) **news**

find some **money**

SB p. 69

MORE Words and Phrases

	superstition	*Many people have superstitions – they believe that something brings good or bad luck.*	Aberglaube
1	**afraid of**	*I know it's stupid, but I'm really afraid of spiders.*	Angst haben vor
	beside	*Some interesting buildings are right beside this river.*	neben
	campfire	*We were sitting around the campfire at night.*	Lagerfeuer
	Don't be silly!		Red keinen Unsinn!
	evil	*I think it's great how she fights evil.*	böse; das Böse
	if	*If you make a wish, it will come true.*	wenn, falls; ob
	mirror	*Does a broken mirror mean bad luck?*	Spiegel
	sleeping bag	*You need to bring a sleeping bag for the camping trip.*	Schlafsack
	spirit	*There is an evil spirit haunting this place.*	Geist
	(be/get) worried	*I'm really starting to get worried now.*	besorgt (sein), sich Sorgen machen
2	cuckoo	*A cuckoo is a kind of bird.*	Kuckuck
4	**Anything else?**	*Will there be anything else, sir?*	Sonst noch was?
	ladder	*You climb up a ladder to get to the roof.*	Leiter
	necklace	*I've got a necklace with a lucky charm on it.*	Halskette
	row	*I never sit in the thirteenth row in the cinema.*	Reihe
	shake	*We shake hands when we meet people for the first time.*	schütteln
	superstitious	*Are you superstitious?*	abergläubisch
	tiger's eye	*In my country, many people wear a tiger's eye around their neck for good luck.*	Tigerauge (Schmuckstein)
	turn round	*She turned round and went back home.*	(sich) umdrehen
5	**hold sb tight(ly)**	*In his dream, a snake was holding him tightly.*	jdn festhalten
	magpie	*A magpie is a kind of bird.*	Elster
	statement	*This statement is not true.*	Äußerung, Aussage
8	**do the dishes**	*I'll do the dishes after dinner.*	(ab-)spülen, abwaschen
9	**catch a cold**	*Take your jacket or you'll catch a cold.*	sich erkälten
	toothbrush	*If you drop your toothbrush in the morning, you'll catch a cold the next day.*	Zahnbürste
G	crack	*The cracks are the lines between the stones.*	Riss, Spalt; hier: Fuge
	pavement (BE)	*I don't walk on cracks in the pavement.*	Gehsteig

UNIT 7 You've got a friend!

Reading

1 **Read the story quickly. What colour is Wendy wearing at the end of it?**

....

I got up in the morning.
"It's a green day", I thought.
I like green days. Other people like green days too.
On green days they all smile.

Anyway, it was a green day. So I put on my dark-green skirt and my light-green sweater.
I put on green nailpolish* and green eyeshadow*. Then I went to school. I stopped at the shop for one of the nice green apples. I met a boy from 4A. His name is Henry Green. So I said, "Hi, Henry," but he just looked at me. Stupid. Then I saw he had brown eyes and I was sorry for saying hi.

I went into my music class. There was a problem. I always sit next to Francine – but Francine was wearing a blue skirt and a white and orange blouse. I just couldn't sit next to her! "Sorry, Francine," I said. "Today I feel like sitting all alone. I think I have a headache."

I believe in colour days, but I don't think other people understand me. They think my colour ideas are a bit funny.

Guess what happened next? Our music teacher came into the class. Behind her was a boy. A new boy. His name was Nate – and he was wearing green jeans, a white and green T-shirt and green running shoes! The teacher looked around and then said, "Why don't you sit next to Wendy, Nate?" So Nate sat down and we became very good friends! That was half a year ago and we're still best friends. But now I must hurry – my orange nail polish isn't dry yet. Nate's waiting. I can see his orange cap outside the window.

VOCABULARY
***nailpolish** – Nagellack
eyeshadow – Lidschatten

SB p. 74, 75

2 How many of these tasks can you do?

1 On green days people feel
- ☐ sad.
- ☐ happy.
- ☐ nervous.

2 Wendy
- ☐ has to wear a uniform to school.
- ☐ takes a bus to school.
- ☐ is allowed to wear make-up at school.

3 Wendy says hello to Henry
- ☐ because of his name.
- ☐ because he's her friend.
- ☐ because she wants to get to know him.

4 Henry says hello to Wendy. T / F

5 Wendy gets a headache in Music. T / F

6 Wendy thinks other people might think her 'colour ideas' are a bit strange. T / F

7 Why do you think Wendy was happy when she saw Nate for the first time?

....

8 How long have Wendy and Nate been friends for?

....

9 What colour would you choose for today and why?

....

3 Check your answers.

Listening

CD4 10

4 Listen to Jack's parents talking about friendship. Then complete the sentences.

1 The most important thing for young people is

....

2 Most young people only have a few

....

3 Tina and Leonie have been best friends since they ....

4 Best friends have known each other ....

5 You hang out with* other friends at ....

6 Best friends tell each other ....

7 With best friends you can talk about ....

VOCABULARY: *hang out with – mit jemandem Zeit verbringen / abhängen

SB p. 74, 75, 77

Essential Grammar Present perfect

5 Match the sentence halves.

1 I've had
2 I have known
3 My father has worked
4 My sister has liked
5 They have lived
6 You have worn
7 I haven't played
8 We have been

☐ in that office for two years.
☐ football since last year.
☐ in that flat since 2004.
☐ Tom since she was 12.
☐ students at this school for a very long time!
☐ my MP3-player since Christmas.
☐ the same shirt for three days.
☐ my best friend for five years.

6 Choose *for* or *since*.

1 I have had my laptop *for* / *since* half a year.
2 Molly has had her cat *for* / *since* December.
3 Ben has had his piano *for* / *since* he was six years old.
4 Mohammed has had his skateboard *for* / *since* three months.
5 Amber has had her roller-skates *for* / *since* yesterday.
6 We have had our dog *for* / *since* six years.
7 We have known Mr Thomas *for* / *since* 2015.
8 I have liked Beyoncé *for* / *since* a long time.

7 Write five sentences that are true for you.

I've had my sunglasses for four months.

	watch		… months.
	computer		… years.
	bike		yesterday.
	roller-skates		the end of the school year.
	snowboard	for	Christmas.
I've had my	earrings		my birthday.
	necklace	since	last summer.
	MP3-player		last year.
	dog		2016.
	sunglasses		… weeks.
	friendship band		… days.

More Grammar Present perfect

8 Write the words in the correct columns. Then add three more examples of your own.

a few weeks	many years	this morning	the weekend
a lifetime	she was a child	three days	10 p.m.
1999	a few seconds	last Friday	a couple of hours

for		
…………	…………	…………
…………	…………	…………
…………	…………	…………

since		
…………	…………	…………
…………	…………	…………
…………	…………	…………

SB p. 79

9 Complete the sentences with the present perfect form of the verbs in the box.

play	wear	be	know	live	be	have	like

1 His wife .... a doctor for twenty years.

2 He .... always .... black clothes since he was a teenager.

3 They .... next door to us for 6 months.

4 You .... my family for a long time.

5 She .... a dog since March.

6 My brother .... mushrooms since he was a baby.

7 Dave .... tennis since he was ten.

8 We .... best friends for years.

10 Complete the sentences about you. Use the present perfect and *for* and *since*.

1 I .... (know my best friend)

2 My family .... (live in our house/flat)

3 I .... (be at this school)

4 My best friend .... (live in this town)

5 I .... (had a mobile phone)

6 Mr/Ms .... (be my English teacher)

11 Complete the dialogues with the correct form of the verbs in brackets.

DIALOGUE 1

Interviewer Hi, Jenny. Tell me, which of the things that you own do you like the most?

Jenny Oh, that's easy. My laptop.

Interviewer Your laptop? OK. How long [1] .... you .... it? (have)

Jenny I [2] .... it since last Christmas. (have)

Interviewer And how often [3] .... you .... it? (use)

Jenny I [4] .... it every day (use). In fact, I [5] .... it right now. (use)

DIALOGUE 2

Interviewer Hi, Roland. Tell me, which of the things that you own do you like the most?

Roland Hmmm, my mobile phone, I suppose.

Interviewer How long [1] .... you .... it? (have)

Roland I [2] .... it for about a month. (have)

Interviewer So, [3] .... you .... it a lot? (use)

Roland Sure, I can play games on it, and take pictures and even videos. I [4] .... a video of my English lesson (take). [5] .... you .... to see it? (want)

SB p. 79

Vocabulary

12 Complete the text. Choose the correct option to complete each space.

Have you heard the news? James has *fallen* [1]………………………… *with* Brenda. No, he hasn't *broken* [2]………………………… *with* her because they weren't girlfriend and boyfriend – although I think she quite likes him. I say that because she really wants to *make* [3]………………………… *with* him. She even tried to say sorry. He wasn't interested. He's really angry with her. The problem started when she said that she didn't like his nose stud. He told her to [4]………………………… *her own business*. I think that was a bit rude. But then she told him to take the stud out. Well, that made him really angry and he [5]………………………… *out of the room*. He hasn't spoken to her for a week now. It's a shame because they were really good friends and *got* [6]………………………… *really well with* each other.

1	a) up	b) out	c) through	**4**	a) take	b) do	c) mind
2	a) up	b) out	c) on	**5**	a) blew	b) rained	c) stormed
3	a) up	b) down	c) over	**6**	a) in	b) on	c) over

13 Match the phrases in italics in 12 with their meanings. Write the numbers next to the letters.

A ☐ to finish a romantic relationship

B ☐ don't give advice* to people if they don't ask you

C ☐ leave somewhere angrily

D ☐ have a good relationship with someone

E ☐ stop talking to a friend

F ☐ become friends again

VOCABULARY: *advice – Ratschlag

14 Match the words to make phrases.

1 lie
2 make fun
3 spend time
4 keep
5 give your brother
6 be honest with
7 become
8 offer someone

☐ friends with the new girl
☐ a secret
☐ something to eat
☐ each other
☐ to your friend
☐ of a classmate
☐ a hard time
☐ with your parents

Developing speaking competencies

15 Complete the mini-dialogues with the missing words.

1 **Sue** What's the [1]m………………………… ? Are you [2]a………………………… ?
Glen I've got a [3]b………………………… of a headache.
Sue [4]P………………………… you. You should take some aspirin.

2 **Mike** You don't look [5]w………………………… at all.
Alison I'm [6]j………………………… a bit tired. I didn't sleep at all last night.
Mike How [7]t………………………… . Why don't you go and lie down for a while?

3 **Andy** What's that on your skin? Your leg looks a bit red.
Gaby It's just a bit of a [8]r………………………… . Actually, it's all over my body.
Andy How [9]a………………………… . You need to see a doctor.

CD4 11

16 Listen and check.

SB p. 76, 78, 80, 81

17 CHOICES

A **Your friend wasn't at the party last night. Send him/her a text message (30–40 words) and ask him/her why he/she wasn't there.**

Ask:

- where he/she was
- why the phone wasn't working
- if you can meet later today

B **Do the following tasks.**

1 Read the task and what a student wrote. What should George let Jessie know?

Task

Your friend just texted you to say he won't be at school today because he/she is feeling bad. You send him/her a message (40–70 words).

In your message:

- ask why he/she is feeling bad
- say what he/she looked like when you last saw him/her
- wish him/her well

From: j.foster@mailconnect.com
Subject: How are you?

REPLY

Hi George,
Sorry to hear you are not well. Is it your headaches again? Or do you think it's the flu? You looked a bit tired yesterday evening after the movie.
I hope you'll feel better in the afternoon.
Let me know how you are, maybe I can drop by.
Take care and have a good rest.
Hugs,
Jessie

Useful phrases:

Asking about health

- How are you?
- Is there anything wrong?
- Are you alright?
- Can I bring you ... ?
- You don't look ... . What's the matter?
- Could it be the flu / something you ate ... ?

2 Now write your own answer to the following task.

Task

You wanted to meet your friend in the evening but you don't feel well. Send him/her a message (40–70 words).

In your message, you tell him/her:

- why you can't meet
- why you don't feel well
- that you hope he/she's OK

SB p. 79

WORD FILE

Relationships

MORE Words and Phrases

	for	*I haven't seen her for years.*	seit
	since	*I haven't spoken to her since then.*	seit
1	laugh at	*Cinema-goers laughed at monsters in films.*	auslachen
	Let's see.	*I think I have the right thing for you. Let's see …*	Moment; also
	make fun of	*Stop making fun of him now! It's enough!*	sich über jdn lustig machen
	move	*When I was 8, we moved to England.*	umziehen, übersiedeln
	soft toy	*I really like all the soft toys on my bed.*	Stofftier, Kuscheltier
	stuff	*Please pack your stuff, we need to go now!*	Zeug
6	**interfere** (with sth)	*Do you sometimes interfere with other people's lives?*	sich (in etwas) einmischen
	Mind your own business.	*That's not your problem. Mind your own business.*	Kümmer dich um deine eigenen Angelegenheiten!
	solve one's problems	*You should try and solve your problems.*	seine Probleme lösen
8	childish	*Laughing at somebody is childish.*	kindisch
	haircut	*After your hair grows too long, you need a haircut.*	Haarschnitt, Frisur
	honest	*Thanks for being honest with me.*	ehrlich
	in the meantime	*Our friends won't be here until later. In the meantime let's have a pizza!*	in der Zwischenzeit, inzwischen
	not either	*I don't like your haircut either.*	auch nicht
	questionnaire	*Fill out the questionnaire.*	Fragebogen
	take it easy	*Take it easy – you'll soon find a good friend.*	sich keinen Stress machen, etwas locker nehmen
	understanding	*Try to be a bit more understanding.*	verständnisvoll
9	script	*Who wrote the script for this film?*	Drehbuch
ME1	**strict**	*Some parents are really strict about going out late.*	streng
	What is it?	*Why are you screaming? What is it?*	Was gibt's?

Reading

1 Read the story.

Hedy Lamarr: A FAMOUS INVENTOR

Hedy Lamarr was a beautiful Hollywood actress*. In the 1940s and 1950s she was the star in over 20 films. But she was also an inventor. She invented the technology that made today's smartphones and GPS possible.

Hedy was born in Vienna in 1914. As a child she always wanted to know how things worked. When she was 18 she married Fritz Mandl. He was an extremely rich man. He had a company that made guns and canons. Hedy was not very happy with her life. So she ran away. In Paris she met the famous film producer Louis B Mayer. He invited her to Hollywood. She started her career as a film star.

Her films were successful, but Hedy found it boring to be an actress. She found the Hollywood lifestyle uninteresting too. She didn't like the parties. She needed a hobby. That's when she started to become an inventor.

One day she met a man called George Antheil. He was also interested in technology. The world was at war*. Hedy was sad because the German submarines were firing torpedoes and destroying ships with children on them. Hedy and George wanted to stop the torpedoes. They invented a system that could block the signals that guided the torpedoes. But for a long time the US military were not interested. They did not believe that such a beautiful actress could be so intelligent. Hedy had to wait for another twenty years to see her idea come true.

In 2014, fourteen years after her death, the National Inventors Hall of Fame added Hedy's name to the list of America's most important inventors.

VOCABULARY
***actress** – Schauspielerin; **war** – Krieg

SB p. 84, 85, 87

2 How many of these tasks can you do?

1 Hedy Lamarr starred in 20 successful films. T / F
2 Hedy worked for a technology company. T / F
3 Hedy was born in Austria. T / F

4 Hedy married a man who
- ☐ was in the film business.
- ☒ had a company that made guns and canons.
- ☐ tried to become rich.

5 Hedy's films were successful,
- ☒ but she found acting boring.
- ☐ and she liked her life in Hollywood.
- ☐ but she wanted her husband with her.

6 Hedy's first invention was
☐ a huge success right away. ☐ not really successful. ☒ well-liked in Hollywood.

7 How did Hedy's inventions stop torpedoes from hitting boats?
....

8 Why was the army not interested in Hedy's invention?
Bec. they didn't belive that she could be so intelligent

9 How do people remember Hedy today?
Her name is on the Hall of Fame

3 Check your answers.

Listening

CD4 12

4 Listen to the talk about Sequoyah (around 1770–1843), a Cherokee Indian. Then complete the sentences below.

1 Sequoyah didn't invent a gadget or a ....
2 He invented an ....
.... Cherokee language.
3 Sequoyah never learned ....
.... when he was young.
4 The Cherokees called books ....
....
5 At first, he used a symbol for ....
....
6 Then he tried to use a symbol for ....
7 In the end he came up with symbols based on ....
....
8 In 1825 a Cherokee .... and in 1828 ....
....
9 Today about .... the language.

VOCABULARY: ***bow and arrow** – Pfeil und Bogen; **the bible** – die Bibel

SB p. 84, 85, 86

Essential Grammar Past simple vs. Present perfect

5 Read the dialogue. Then circle T (*True*) or F (*False*).

Chris Could I borrow some money from you?

Tom You still haven't paid back the money you borrowed from me last week.

Chris What? I didn't borrow any money from you last week.

Tom Yes, you did. Remember? When you bought that Jennifer Lawrence DVD.

Chris Oh, yes. You're right. I needed a present for Jenny.

Tom What? You've given it to her? I wanted to watch it.

1 Chris needs some money. T / F

2 Chris owes Tom some money from yesterday. T / F

3 Chris has forgotten about the money. T / F

4 Chris bought a film with the money. T / F

5 Chris still has the film. T / F

6 Tom hasn't seen the film. T / F

6 Match the questions and the answers.

1 Have you ever been to Spain?
2 Has June finished her homework?
3 Have they found their cat?
4 Has he written you an email?
5 Have they found a new house?
6 Has the film started yet?

[ ] Yes, she finished ten minutes ago.
[ ] No, but he phoned me.
[ ] Yes, and it's a very nice house.
[ ] Yes, we went to Madrid last year.
[ ] Yes, it started about 15 minutes ago.
[ ] Yes, it was in the garden.

7 Choose the correct option to complete the sentences.

1 My sister *got* / *has got* married last Sunday.
2 She *met* / *has met* her husband three years ago.
3 I *didn't* / *haven't* met a famous person in my life.
4 Jacqueline's sad because she *has just broken* / *just broke* up with her boyfriend.
5 My team *lost* / *has lost* the cup final 2–0 last night.
6 I'm sorry, Robert's not in. He *has just gone* / *just went* to the shops.
7 The flight from Belfast *has already* / *already* arrived.
8 The flight from Dublin *arrived* / *has arrived* more than an hour ago.

SB p. 88

More Grammar Past simple vs. Present perfect

8 **Complete with the past simple or present perfect forms of the words in brackets.**

I [1] .... (always be) interested in inventing something. Two years ago I [2] .... (invent) the automatic-reply-to-your-parents machine. You could sit in the living room with it and press a button and the machine would say in your voice things like "uhu, hmmm, aha, yeah fine". It really works. I [3] .... (try) it a million times, believe me.

I [4] .... (not have) a good idea for some time, but yesterday I [5] .... (have) a brilliant one. I [6] .... (come up) with this new homework writer. All you do is feed it some paper. Then press *Article* or *Story* or *Letter* or *Email*. Put in a few key words – and it writes your text. I [7] .... (already try) with my English homework. It [8] .... (work). My teacher says it's the best story he [9] ....(ever read)!

9 **Complete with the words from the box in the correct tense.**

invent ~~see~~ take see think say transport not watch answer

I [1] ....have.......... just ....seen.......... such a stupid movie. It was about a guy who [2] .... time machines for different distances in time. So, for example, the blue one was for up to 200 years in the past, the red one [3] .... you back 2,000 years, the yellow one [4] .... you back only for a day. It was complete chaos.

"[5] .... anybody ever .... about the script?" I asked my friend Tony. "And [6] .... the director ever .... the movie?" Tony [7] .... , "It's all about running to the wrong machines and going back to the wrong time, because people can't remember the colour codes." "See?" I [8] .... "Why [9] .... you .... your movie before you showed it to us?" I asked him.

10 **Complete the dialogues with the correct forms of the verbs in brackets.**

1 **A** .... you .... (be) to Italy?
B Yes, I .... (go) there last year.
A Which cities .... you .... (visit)?
B We .... (visit) Rome and Naples. We .... (have) a great time.

2 **A** .... you .... (meet) a famous person?
B Yes, I .... (meet) Bill Gates when I was 12.
A Wow! What .... you .... (say) to him?
B I .... (ask) him for some money.

11 **Write two more dialogues using these first lines.**

1 Have you ever found a lot of money?

2 Have you ever had a bad accident?

SB p. 88

Vocabulary

12 Unscramble the following words.

1 vnient ....
2 idecsvor ....
3 sdgnei ....
4 xepemeritn ....
5 mpiover ....
6 dproecu ....

13 Complete with the correct form of the words in the box.

invent
work out
try it out
experiment
discover
improve
design
find
produce

I 1.......... the plans for the spaceship by accident. Somebody called Helen R. 2.......... a hyper-hyper drive. I don't know how she 3.......... the science but she did. And she 4.......... the most beautiful spaceship I've ever seen. She 5.......... with the hyper-hyper drive for years. And every year she 6.......... it a bit. If she ever 7.......... it, I really want to 8.......... with her. That is, if I ever 9.......... her.

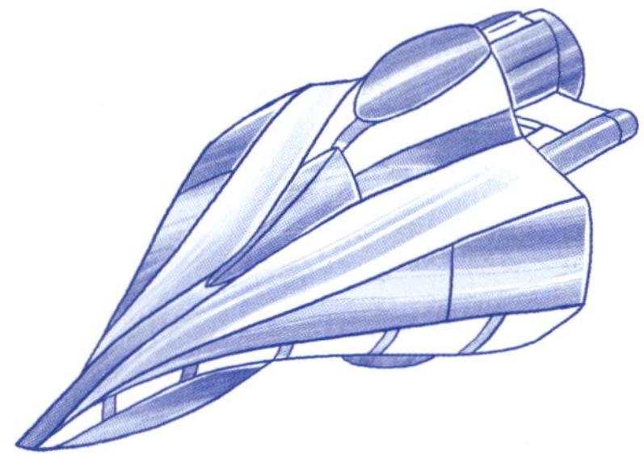

14 Do the crossword puzzle.

Down:
1 a method to find out if something works
2 to come up with something new
4 to find out

Across:
3 to make
5 to make something better
6 to test to see if it is useful
7 to create a pattern

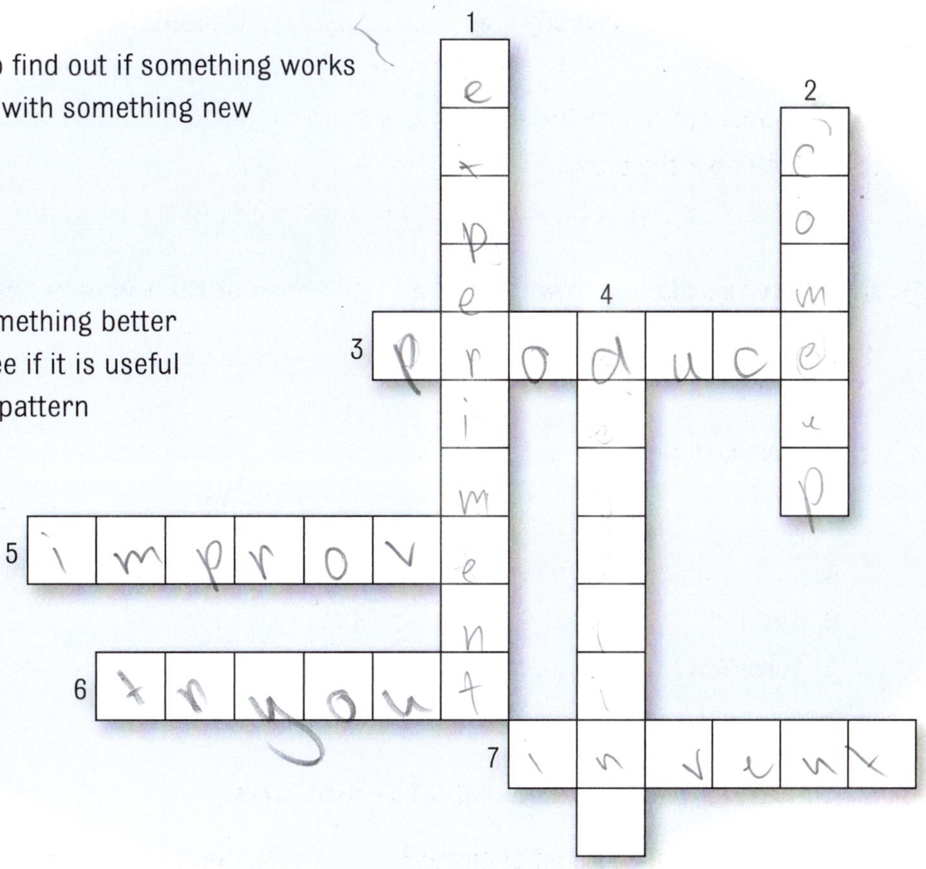

SB p. 85

Developing writing skills Description

15 CHOICES

A **Describe your school building to a friend (40–70 words).**
Say:

- how big it is
- how old it is
- how it looks from outside
- how many (class)rooms there are
- what your classroom looks like
- which room is your favourite room

B **Do the following tasks.**

1 **Read the task and what a student wrote. How many objects are there on how many floors?**

Task **Imagine you have been to a museum and have to write a description (120–180 words) of that museum. Write about:**

- where the museum is and what history it has
- how big it is and what you can see there
- your favourite object
- how much time you spent there

Last week our school went to the Science Museum in London. It is in South Kensington and it is a massive old building. Originally the science collection was in a museum across the road, but in 1862 it moved into the building that is now the Science Museum. It is one of London's top attractions and more than 3 million people visit it every year. There are more than 300,000 items on four floors. Some items are very famous, such as the early steam trains or the first jet engine or the Clock of the Long Now that keeps time for 10,000 years. There are also good shows on medical history, and in 2014 a gallery on the Information Age opened. There are many more galleries, and they are all very interesting. One of my favourite objects is Eric, England's first robot. He was built in 1928 and has been recreated for the Science Museum. Eric can talk and move – in a mechanical way. We spent half a day at the Science Museum, but you need days to see everything.

SB p. 88

Language tip: Making paragraphs

Use paragraphs to help structure your text. Each one should focus on one idea (or maybe two connected ideas). When you want to focus on a new idea, start a new paragraph. This is important because it makes it easier for the reader to understand the text.

It's a good idea to use bullet points in the task to help you organise your paragraphs. Think which of the points can be made into a single paragraph.

2 Look at the text and the bullet points in 1 again. Use bullet points to help you divide the text into four paragraphs. Put a ⌐ to show the start of a new paragraph.

Writing tip:

Writing a description

When writing a description, think carefully about:

- how many facts you include – remember the word limit
- how much detail you want to include
- the technical or special vocabulary you want to use
- who your readers are

3 Now write your own answer to the following task.

Task

Write a description of a house – either your house or the house of a person you know (120–180 words). Write about:

- where the house is and what it looks like
- how big it is and what kind of rooms there are
- what furniture is in the rooms
- your favourite room

Everyday English Bad hair day

DVD Complete the dialogues with the phrases on p. 89 in your Student's Book.

1 A Dad says he's going to buy a new television – maybe next month.
B .... This TV's terrible!

2 A Jane, have you heard? You got top marks in the Maths test.
B ....
A No. I heard Mr Cooper telling someone and he's the Maths teacher, so he should know, shouldn't he?

3 **Dad** Jamie, please don't go out wearing those awful clothes!
Jamie Oh, Dad. .... These clothes are totally cool!

4 A OK. One more cup and then the washing-up's done!
B Well, ... We've still got to wash the glasses.

WORD FILE

Inventions

MORE Words and Phrases

	invention	*One of the world's most important inventions is probably the wheel.*	Erfindung
	inventor	*One day, I want to be a famous inventor, like Steve Jobs.*	Erfinder/in
1	broadcast	*They're going to broadcast the experiment live tomorrow.*	übertragen, senden
	cheap	*If he needed some, I'd lend my friend some money and buy myself a cheaper bike.*	billig
	detect	*They've detected a new source of water in the forest.*	finden
	develop	*He developed a new communication system.*	entwickeln
	energy	*Your old dishwasher uses a lot of energy – you should get a new one.*	Energie; Strom
	influence	*Marie Curie's findings had a great influence on today's medicine.*	Einfluss
	invent	*He's still trying to invent a flying car.*	erfinden
	invest	*Many companies are investing in new technologies.*	investieren, Geld anlegen
	power	*There's no power running through this cable.*	hier: Strom
	responsible for	*This company is responsible for the oil spill.*	verantwortlich für
3	discover	*The scientists discovered a bag of gold in the cave.*	entdecken
	improve	*The best way to improve your French is to live in France.*	verbessern
	work sth out	*It took us some time, but we finally worked out the solution.*	herausfinden, erarbeiten
4	impressed	*I saw the new 'Star Wars' film and I was really impressed.*	beeindruckt
9	**own**	*Do you own a pet? Is it a dog or a cat?*	besitzen
10	crutches	*I have broken my leg and now need crutches to help me walk.*	Krücken
	ramp	*You can get into the building by using the stairs or the ramp.*	Rampe
	walker	*My granny is quite old so she uses a walker.*	Gehhilfe
	wheelchair	*After the accident he had to use a wheelchair for a couple of weeks.*	Rollstuhl
11	award	*Who won the Songwriter of the Year Award?*	Preis, Auszeichnung
13	**cost**	*My mum's car cost a lot.*	kosten
ME1	shelf (pl shelves)	*She dusted the shelves and everything.*	Regal
ME4	**How about …?**	*How about signing a petition?*	Wie wäre es mit …?

Reading

1 **Read the text about a 14-year-old Australian teenager.**

Australian adventures

Hi, my name's Brett. My family, that's Mum, Dad and me, live in Broome, Western Australia. Western Australia is about 80 times larger than Italy, but only 2.6 million people live there.

Both my parents work. My dad is a mechanic* and my mum is a nurse*. I often help my father at the weekends when he repairs* cars for friends. When we drive out into the bush, Dad often lets me drive. Of course, I am not allowed to drive in town.

At the weekends I often go fishing or swimming with my friends or my parents. From October to March we don't go swimming because there may be box jellyfish in the water. The box jellyfish is one of the most deadly jellyfish. In Australia, they killed up to 70 people during the last 100 years. If they sting you, the best thing to do is to put vinegar* on the skin. That's why we always take a bottle of vinegar with us.

A year ago I went camping in the bush with my friend Shaun and his dad. Suddenly at 3 o'clock in the morning we felt something pulling on our tent. We were very scared. Shaun's dad turned the torch on and we quickly got out of the tent* and ran to the car. Shaun's dad started the car and in the headlights* we could see a big crocodile that was pulling the tent into the river. We were really shocked and drove straight home.

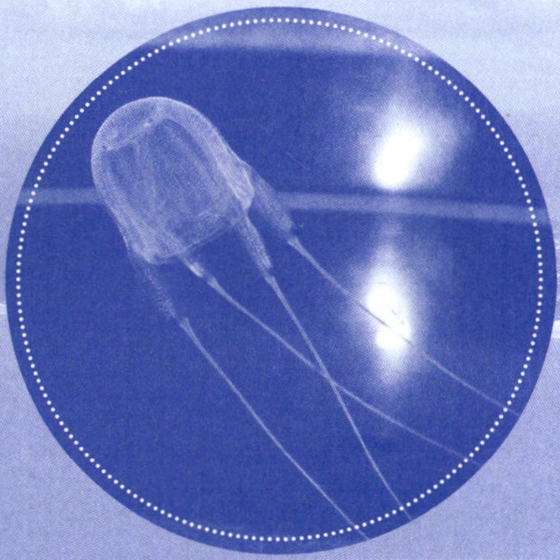

VOCABULARY: ***mechanic** – Mechaniker/in; **nurse** – Krankenpfleger/in; **repair** – reparieren; **vinegar** – Essig; **tent** – Zelt; **headlights** – Scheinwerferlicht

SB p. 92, 93

2 How many of these tasks can you do?

Complete the sentences with no more than 4 words.

1 The population of Western Australia ....
2 His parents' jobs are a mother nurse, dad mechanic .
3 Brett is allowed to drive his father's car when they are
in the bush .

4 It's dangerous to go swimming at Christmas. T / F (F circled)
5 Drinking vinegar helps with box jellyfish stings. T / F (F circled)
6 Brett and his friend went camping by the sea. T / F (T circled)

7 What did Brett feel in the middle of the night when he was camping?
something pulling the tent
8 What did they do immediately?
The dad turned the toch on
9 What did they see in the car headlights?
a big crocodile

3 Check your answers.

Listening

CD4 13

4 Listen and write the countries under the photos.

Hi, I'm José and I'm from Peru .

My name's Agripina and I'm from Bolivia .

Hey. My name's Renato and I'm from South Amerika Brasil .

My name's Raukani and I'm from [illegible] .

CD4 13

5 Listen again. Write *Raukani*, *Renato*, *Agripina* or *José*.

1 Who doesn't go to school? Raukani
2 Who lives at a high altitude*? Bolivia
3 Who helps his father grow things to eat?
José
4 Who likes water sports? Renato
5 Who travels by water? Raukani
6 Who gets angry about pollution*?
Renato
7 Who doesn't live with his/her sister?
José
8 Who looks after animals?
Bolivia

VOCABULARY: ***altitude** – Meereshöhe; **water plants** – Pflanzen gießen; **pollution** – Umweltverschmutzung

SB p. 92, 93, 94

Essential Grammar *be allowed to / let*

6 Match the signs and the sentences.

1  [F]

2  [A]

3  [D]

4  [C]

5  [E]

6  [B]

A You aren't allowed to park your car here.
B You aren't allowed to swim here.
C You aren't allowed to walk on the grass.
D You aren't allowed to go in here.
E You aren't allowed to eat food in here.
F You aren't allowed to take photographs.

7 Match the questions and answers.

1 Are you allowed to invite your friends over?
2 Do your parents let you come home late?
3 Do your parents let you have parties at home?
4 Does your dad let you drive his car?
5 Do your parents let you surf the internet?
6 Are you allowed to have a pet at home?

[4] Of course he doesn't. I'm only 12.
[5] Yes, but I'm not allowed to go into chat rooms.
[6] No, because my dad hates animals.
[2] Yes, but I have to be back by 9 p.m. on Mondays to Thursdays.
[1] Yes, but we're not allowed to make too much noise.
[3] Yes, they do if I promise to tidy up after.

8 Write your own answers to the questions in 7.

9 Put the dialogue in order.

[5] **A** Yes, Fridays and Saturdays too.
[1] **A** Are you allowed to come home late?
[3] **A** Yes, but I have to be home by 10 p.m. every night.
[2] **B** Yes, but only at the weekends. Do your parents let you stay out late?
[6] **B** Wow. Your parents are strict.
[4] **B** What! Even on Saturdays?

SB p. 98, 99

More Grammar *be allowed to / let*

10 **Draw two signs for your bedroom door and write a sentence under each one to explain what they mean.**

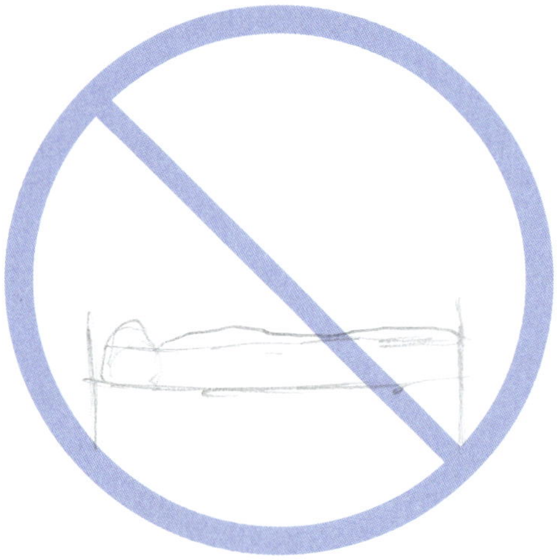

1 You are not allowed to sit or lay down in my bed

2 You are not allowed to eat in my room

11 **Complete with the correct forms of *be allowed to.***

"On the school trip, you [1] won't be allowed (not allow) to stay up later than 10 o'clock," our teacher said. "And you [2] are not allowed (not allow) to get together in one room and make a lot of noise." That was before the trip, but during the trip it was even worse. We [3] are not allowed (not allow) to use our mobile phones for games and we [4] not allowed (not allow) to listen to music during meals. "Is there anything we [5] are allowed (allow) to do?" I asked the teacher. "I'll think about it," he said. "Ask me again next week." I think teachers like him shouldn't [6] allow (allow) to go on school trips.

12 **Write sentences using the correct form of *be allowed to.***

1 James ✓ watch TV / ✗ not watch TV after 10 o'clock.
James is allowed to watch TV, but he isn't allowed to watch TV after 10 o'clock.

2 Sarah ✓ go to bed late / ✗ not get up late.
Sahra is allowed to go to bed late, but she isn't allowed to get up late

3 We ✓ wear jeans to school / ✗ not wear shorts.
We are allowed to wear jeans to school, but we are not allowed to wear shorts.

4 They ✓ listen to music / ✗ not listen without headphones.
They are allowed to listen to music, but they aren't allowed to listen without headphones

5 I ✓ go to my friend's house / ✗ not stay for the night.
I am allowed to go to my friendshouse, but I am not allowed to stay for the night

6 She ✓ have parties at home / ✗ not play loud music.
She is allowed to have parties at home, but she is not allowed to play loud music.

SB p. 99

13 **Rewrite the sentences in 12 using *let*.**

1 James' parents let him watch TV, but they don't let him watch it after 10 o'clock.
2 Sarah's dad let her go to bed late, but they don't let her get up late
3 The headmaster let them wear jeans to school, but don't let them wear shorts
4 Mum let them to listen to music, but they don't let them play loud music.
5 Dad let me go to my friends house, but he don't let me not stay for the night
6 Her parents let her have parties at home, but don't let her play loud music

14 **Look back at 9. Then write similar dialogues for the questions below.**

1 A Are you allowed to borrow your dad's camcorder?
B Yes, but I have to be carefully.
A Yes, but only at the weekends. Do your parent's let you?
B That's great

2 A Do your parents let you buy your own clothes?
B Yes, but with my own money. Do your parent's let you?
A Yes, but I should not spend to much.
B We should really go together (shopping).

Vocabulary

15 **Match the parts that go together.**

1	dye	3	too many sweets
2	turn up	6	your bike to school
3	eat	1	your hair
4	watch	5	your own clothes
5	buy	2	your music really loud
6	ride	4	TV all day long

16 **Find 13 activities in the word snake.**

dyeyour|hair|getatattoo|goroller skating without pads|buy your own clothes|have a party at home|use your parents' camcorder|go to the disco|come home after ten at the weekend|turn your music up really loud|get a nose stud|play video games all day|watch TV after 10 o'clock|eat too many sweets

17 Which of the activities from 16 are these people doing?

They're having a party at home.

The music is really loud. The girl is driving roller skates without anything down the staircase. Two kids are watching TV. Two boy's are playing a videogame. One boy is eating candy the other one is drinking something

Developing speaking competencies

18 Put the words in order to make offers.

1 some / I / lend / could / you ……………………

2 I / brother / his / ask / my / Why / to / don't / you / lend

……………………

3 you / like / Would / you / me / with / to / come

……………………

4 want / you / here / me / have / you / can / to / ask / my / Do / mum / if / it

……………………

19 Write the offers from 18 into the correct mini-dialogues.

1 **Fred** I want to get a nose stud but I'm a bit afraid.
Donna ……………………
Fred Would you? I'd feel much braver.

2 **Jack** I want to go roller-skating but I can't find my pads.
Lana ……………………
Jack Really? That's so kind of you.

3 **May** Mum won't let me have a birthday party at home.
James ……………………
May That would be really nice. Thank you.

4 **Liz** Mum said I can buy my own clothes for the party but she didn't give me any money.
Andy ……………………
Liz Really? What would I do without you?

CD4 14

20 Listen and check.

SB p. 100, 101

21 CHOICES

A Write an email (40–60 words) to a friend in which you offer to go shopping for a party. Ask him/her:

- how many people are going to the party
- what they want you to buy
- how much money they want to spend

B Do the following tasks.

1 Read the task and what a student wrote. When can Martin meet?

Task Your friend David asked you to get together with a few others for a Maths study group. You send him an email (40–70 words) about the idea.

In your email:

- say when you have time
- say where you could meet
- offer to organise a few things

From: martin_h@mailconnect.com
Subject: Maths study group
REPLY

Hi David,
About that study group for Maths. I could meet tomorrow afternoon with you all. Why don't we use one of the empty classrooms? Would you like me to bring the books or will you? And do you want me to check out if it's OK to use a classroom?
Looking forward to our first meeting.
Martin

Useful language:

Making offers

- I could …
- Why don't I … ?
- Let me …
- If you want me to … , I can …
- It's no problem for me to …
- Can I get you … ?

2 Now write your own answer to the following task.

Task Your friend Hanna asked you to help her with moving her things to her new flat. Write her an email (40–70 words).

In your email:

- say when you have time
- say who else you/she could ask for help
- offer to organise a few things

SB p. 99

WORD FILE

Teen activities

MORE Words and Phrases

2b	hang out	*We like to hang out at the youth club.*	herumhängen
	housewife (pl housewives)	*Her mother looks after their home. She is a housewife.*	Hausfrau
	mix	*In Apartheid black and white people weren't allowed to mix.*	vermischen
3	**clear** the snow	*In winter you have to clear the snow in front of your house.*	Schnee räumen
	deer (pl deer)	*Sometimes we go hunting for deer.*	Hirsch, Reh
	dentist	*A dentist looks after your teeth.*	Zahnarzt/Zahnärztin
	grizzly bear	*The grizzly bear is the biggest and strongest bear in America.*	Grizzlybär
	housework	*I don't have to do any housework.*	Hausarbeit
5	**shoot**	*A crazy fan shot John Lennon.*	schießen; hier: erschießen
6	back seat	*He was trying to hide in the back seat.*	Rücksitz, Rückbank
	border	*We crossed the border from Mexico.*	Grenze
8	**pay attention**	*Pay attention in class!*	aufpassen; Acht geben
	tattoo	*I'm not allowed to get a tattoo.*	Tätowierung
9	**salesman / saleswoman**	*Her mother is a saleswoman.*	Verkäufer/in
10	earring	*You have really nice earrings.*	Ohrring
	stud	*Look, he's got a stud in his nose.*	Stecker, hier: Piercing
11	fake	*It's not real, it's fake.*	falsch, gefälscht
13	be grounded	*I am grounded because I came home late.*	Hausarrest haben
G	drill for oil	*They are drilling for oil in Antarctica.*	nach Öl bohren
ME1	changing room	*The changing rooms are over there.*	Umkleidekabine
	lend	*Tony lends Sally £15.*	leihen

Reading

1 Read the story.

The computer lab protest

We've got this new computer lab at our school, but we do not often go there. The older students go to the lab all the time. They can even play online games there. We can never go to the lab without a teacher. That's unfair!

So I went to see the headmaster. My friends came too. He said, "Sorry, guys. Talk to the computer teachers about the situation."

So we talked to the teachers. "Sorry guys," they said. "Talk to the headmaster."

So I organised a meeting of all the 13-year-olds in our school. We discussed the situation and made a plan: Younger students should be allowed to use the lab too. One of us should be a 'labbie'. The labbie checks that everything is in order and nobody breaks things. We took the plan to the headmaster. He said, "I'll think about it." After two weeks we went to see him again, and again he said, "I'll think about it."

So we had another meeting. "Let's protest in front of the computer lab," I said.

Five minutes later we were standing in front of the lab with signs in our hands: *Let us into the lab!* and *Computer time is not a crime.*

Ten minutes later the headmaster was there. "I promise you a meeting next Friday. Then we can find a solution," he said.

Next Friday we had the meeting. "You can use the computer lab too. Some of the older kids will be computer labbies for three hours every afternoon," the headmaster said.

And of course we're really happy now!

SB p. 104, 105

2 How many of these tasks can you do?

1 The writer can never use the computer lab. T / F

2 Students can only use the computer room for learning. T / F

3 The writer spoke to the headmaster first about the problem. T / F

4 At the first meeting the students
- ☐ organised a protest.
- ☐ discussed what to do.
- ☐ played about and broke things.

5 A labbie is someone who
- ☐ uses a lab a lot.
- ☐ works in a lab.
- ☐ looks after a lab.

6 At the second meeting the students
- ☐ organised a protest.
- ☐ invited the headmaster along to discuss things.
- ☐ got very angry.

7 Why did the headmaster promise the kids a meeting on Friday?

....

8 What suggestion did the headmaster make?

....

9 What one thing would you like most to change in your school and why?

....

3 Check your answers.

Listening

CD4 15

4 Read the letter to the headmaster and then listen to the conversation. Find four differences in the letter and underline them.

Dear Mr Owens,

We are writing to ask you to think again about the end-of-year party. As you know, this is a very popular event. All the school leavers* love it. We understand that last year there was some trouble and some of the boys did not behave* very well. We know that three windows were broken and we understand that you don't want this to happen again. But you don't have to stop our party. That was last year's school leavers, not us. We are asking you to change your mind, please. If you say that we can't have our party, then we will have to organise a protest march. We are sure that all the students in all the years will join. Please remember that two years ago my brother organised a protest about the school library and it worked. We are sure that you don't want something like that to happen again.

Thank you for your attention.

Julian Harvey

VOCABULARY: *school leaver – Schulabgänger/in; **behave** – sich benehmen

SB p. 104, 105, 107

Essential Grammar *be able to / allowed to*

5 Look at what happened yesterday. Write the children's names under the pictures.

Yesterday ...

- Jill wasn't able to go to school.
- Joanna wasn't allowed to buy the dress.
- James wasn't able to phone his friend.
- Sue wasn't able to get into the garden.
- Lucy and Andy weren't able to ride their bikes.
- Mark and Ron weren't allowed to play.

1 She wasn't able to get into the garden

2 Jill wasn't able to go to school

3 Mark and Ron weren't allowed to play.

4 Joanna wasn't allowed to buy the dress.

5 Lucy and Andy weren't able to ride their bikes

6 Jame wasn't able to phone his friend

6 What do they want for tomorrow? Read the sentences. Who says each one?

Tomorrow I hope ...

1. We'll be able to go for a ride. — Lucy and Andy
2. I'll be able to get into that garden. — Mark and Ron
3. I'll be able to get some money from Dad. — Joanna
4. We'll be able to finish our game. — Sue
5. I'll be able to talk to Jim. — Jame
6. I'll be able to get out of bed. — Jill

More Grammar *be able to* (mixed tenses)

7 Underline the correct form of *be able to*.

1. I *won't be able* / *wasn't able* to do my homework tonight. I haven't got time.
2. He spoke so fast. I *won't be able* / *wasn't able* to understand anything he said.
3. They got the visa. They *were allowed* / *weren't allowed* to enter the country.
4. She *was able* / *has been able* to stop the man and the police arrested him last night.
5. I *won't be allowed* / *will be allowed* to come to your party next Friday. I'm sorry.
6. We *weren't able* / *won't be able* to go to the cinema because we didn't have enough money.
7. I'm sorry I *wasn't able* / *haven't been able* to write to you for such a long time.

8 Complete the sentences so they are true for you.

1. So far this year I have been able to ....
2. Last night I was able to ....
3. One day I hope I'll be able to ....
4. My best friend isn't allowed to ....
5. I'm very lucky because I'm able to ....
6. Today I haven't been able to ....
7. This weekend I won't be able to ....
8. When I was five I wasn't allowed to ....

9 Put the dialogue in order.

- [ ] **A** Exactly! Work's going to start next month. Are you able to help me?
- [ ] **A** We want to start a petition and hand out leaflets to all the people in the village.
- [1] **A** You weren't at the meeting last night.
- [ ] **A** They're planning to build a motorway through our village.
- [ ] **B** That's a stupid idea. Our kids won't be able to walk to school safely any more.
- [ ] **B** Yes, I'm sorry. I wasn't able to make it. What was it about?
- [ ] **B** Of course. I'm able to do whatever you need.

10 Choose one of the situations below and write a short dialogue. Use the dialogue in 9 to help you.

There are plans to build a supermarket where the tennis courts* are.

VOCABULARY: *court – Platz

The school library is not open any more in the afternoon.

SB p. 110

Vocabulary

11 Match the sentence halves.

1 Would you like to sign
2 We're going
3 Can you help us hand
4 Have you thought about sending
5 We need to organise

[5] a meeting to see how people feel about this.
[3] out leaflets in the High Street on Friday?
[4] out emails telling people about the problem?
[2] on a protest march against the war tomorrow.
[1] this petition against animal cruelty?

12 Complete the sentences with the words in the box.

distances	plastic bags	recycle	locally produced	litter bugs	save

1 It is very important to ...save... water.
2 You should really buy ...locally produced... food.
3 I never take ...plastic bags... at my food store.
4 We always ...recycle... glass bottles and take them to the bottle bank.
5 Only ...litter bugs... leave bottles and cans on the beach.
6 People shouldn't drive short ...distances... , they should use their bikes or walk.

13 Look at the pictures. Write sentences about what these people *should / shouldn't* do.

1 He should buy locally produced apples.

2 She shouldn't leave bottles or paper on the ground

3 He shouldn't drope his drink on the floor

4 She shouldn't put the bottle in another container

5 She shouldn't take plastic bags

6 She shouldn't waste water

SB p. 106, 108, 109

14 CHOICES

A **Design a leaflet for an evening of music by the school band.**

In your leaflet:

- say when and where it takes place
- say who is invited
- give 2–3 examples of songs the school band will play

B **Do the following tasks.**

1 **Read the task and what a student wrote. How much is it to go to the party?**

Task

Someone asked you to design a leaflet for a school party. On your leaflet say:

- where and when the party is
- who is invited
- what the entertainment is
- what food and drink there is
- how much it is to go

Trentdale Comprehensive School
End of Year Party
Where: school playground
When: 6 p.m. to 8 p.m.
Parents, teachers, school children are all invited.
There will be games!
There will be a band!
There will be singing and dancing!
Sandwiches, cakes and drinks are free.
Free entry – but we are happy for donations!
See you at our party!

SB p. 110

Language tip:

Layout

For a leaflet a good layout is important because it needs to attract the reader's attention:

- Use a full page. Think how to best spread your text/pictures over it.
- Try not to leave large white spaces at the bottom or the top of the page.
- Think how you can use different fonts and font sizes to highlight important information and to draw attention to your leaflet.

2 Look at the leaflet and write on it where and how you would improve it. (For example: Make "See you at our party" larger and bold it.)

Writing tip:

Writing a leaflet

- Write your leaflet by hand first.
- Use short sentences.
- Use good slogans (e.g. SOS – Save Our School).
- Use words and phrases that are easy to remember (e.g. words starting with the same letter – *Help with Homework?*).
- If possible, design your leaflet on a computer.

3 Now write your own answer to the following task.

Task

Someone asked you to design a leaflet for a school play. On your leaflet say:

- what the title of the play is
- where and when the play takes place
- who is invited
- how to get tickets
- how much it is to go

Everyday English Girls and football

DVD **Look at the phrases on p. 111 in your Student's Book again. Use them to complete the dialogues.**

1 A .... ? Steve's going out with Julie now.

B .... He was always looking at her.

2 A My dad's bought a Harley Davidson motorbike.

B .... ! Can we go for a ride on it?

A .... ! He won't even take me out on it, so he certainly won't take you!

SB p. 110, 111

WORD FILE

Getting the message across

to **sign a petition**
to **go on a protest march**
to **send out emails**
to **hand out leaflets**
to **organise a meeting**

Being green

to **save water**
to **buy locally produced food**
to **recycle** (glass bottles)
Don't **take plastic bags** at your food store.
Don't **drop litter**.
Don't **leave** bottles or cans in the park.
Don't **drive short distances**.

MORE Words and Phrases

1	hand out	*Let's hand out leaflets.*	austeilen, verteilen
	leaflet	*They read the leaflet and decided to go on the protest march.*	Prospekt/Flugblatt
	organise, organize (AE)	*We have to get organised.*	organisieren, koordinieren
2	**be able to do**	*Our kids won't be able to play here.*	tun können
	city council	*Let's write emails to the city council.*	Stadtrat
	multi-storey car park	*They want to build a multi-storey car park near our road.*	mehrstöckiges Parkhaus
	rumour	*The rumours about the car park are true.*	Gerücht
4	chairman (pl chairmen)	*The chairman is the leader of the council.*	Vorsitzende/r; Vorstand
	come up with a solution	*It's sometimes difficult to come up with a solution that everyone likes.*	eine Lösung finden
	send out sth	*Let's send out emails to all the students.*	etwas versenden, verschicken
7	**sign sth**	*Please sign this petition to help save the bees.*	etwas unterschreiben
9a	**democracy**	*In a democracy, people vote for their political leaders.*	Demokratie
	environment	*You can save water to protect the environment.*	Umgebung; hier: Umwelt
	movement	*She started the Green Belt movement in Kenya.*	Bewegung
9b	**arrest**	*One way to escape arrest is to go abroad.*	Verhaftung
	decision	*She made the right decision.*	Entscheidung
	public	*I was allowed to go to public high school.*	öffentlich
	refuse	*Rosa Parks refused to give up her seat on a bus to a white man.*	ablehnen, sich weigern
	tired of	*Rosa Parks was tired of getting up again and again for white people.*	es Leid sein, etwas satt haben
10	close down	*The company closed down a month later.*	schließen
	heroine	*She's a real heroine.*	Heldin
12	litter bug	*Don't be a litter bug!*	Umweltverschmutzer/in
ME1	**ridiculous**	*A motorway through the village? That's ridiculous!*	lächerlich
ME3	**fix**	*Can you fix my computer?*	reparieren

UNIT 11 California Dreaming

Reading

1 Read about California.

Why do millions of visitors go to California every year? We asked some tourists why they were here. This is what we found out.

Many people love the cities in California. Carl from Germany said that for him San Francisco and Los Angeles are two of the best cities in the world. But the smaller towns are attractive too. June Woo Kim thinks Monterey and Carmel are great for shopping.

Shaun and Debbie from Australia think that California has got great beaches and that they're as good as the beaches back home.

Many tourists like California's beautiful nature. Some visitors from Europe for example like the coast north of San Francisco very much. Many European tourists also like cities like Santa Rosa north of San Francisco better than the big cities.

But everyone agreed on one thing: Californian people are very friendly. That is why many tourists say they will come back to California again!

SB p. 114, 116, 117

2 How many of these tasks can you do?

1 Carl thinks that San Francisco and Los Angeles can disappoint some tourists. T / F

2 Monterey and Carmel are examples of smaller Californian towns. T / F

3 Shaun and Debbie think Californian beaches are better than Australian beaches. T / F

Complete the sentences with no more than 4 words.

4 Many European visitors think .... of San Francisco is great.

5 Santa Rosa is ....

6 Tourists say that the people from California are ....

7 Why do many tourists want to come back to California?

....

8 What part of California would you like to visit most and why?

....

9 Why do you think most tourists come to Austria?

....

3 Check your answers.

Listening

CD4 16

4 Listen. Which of these bridges does Billy cross to get to work?

☐ Golden Gate Bridge

☐ Bay Bridge

CD4 16

5 Listen again and choose the correct answer.

1 Billy is in the UK to
- ☐ spend time with his family.
- ☐ do some work for his company.
- ☐ organise his move to San Francisco.

2 How many times does Billy cross the Bay Bridge for work every week?
- ☐ 3 ☐ 4 ☐ 6

3 Why does Anne want to go to San Francisco?
- ☐ to see the Golden Gate Bridge
- ☐ because she's got friends living there
- ☐ because it always looks good in the films

4 What does Billy like about his journey to work?
- ☐ the roads have little traffic
- ☐ the view
- ☐ the weather

5 Why does Billy never get tired of* living in San Francisco?
- ☐ because loads of good bands play there
- ☐ because there's lots of things to do there
- ☐ because it's cheap

6 What does Anne want Billy to do?
- ☐ invite her to his house in San Francisco
- ☐ find her work at his company
- ☐ show her some photos of California

VOCABULARY: *get tired of something – einer Sache müde/überdrüssig werden

SB p. 116, 117, 118

Essential Grammar Present perfect continuous

6 Match the sentences and the pictures.

1. They look tired. They've been running for three hours.
2. He's been watching TV all night.
3. She's been waiting for twenty minutes.
4. He's been talking on his mobile for an hour.
5. They've been practising this song for a long time.
6. She's been dreaming of a new mountain bike for months.
7. You've been chasing cats again!
8. He's only been playing for a month.

7 Match the sentences.

1. It has been raining all day.
2. I have been shopping for presents.
3. He has been working as a waiter for two months.
4. She has been looking after the two children since April.
5. They have been waiting for the doctor for an hour.
6. I have been studying for the test for three days.

[3] That's why you haven't seen him for a while.
[4] That's why she's so tired.
[5] That's why they're so bored.
[1] That's why we haven't been outside today.
[6] That's why you haven't seen me online recently.
[2] That's why I haven't got any money to buy you a coffee.

More Grammar Present perfect continuous

8 Put the verbs in brackets into the correct form of the present perfect continuous.

1. **A** Why are you so tired?
   B I ....have been working.... very hard. (work)
2. **A** Please put the phone down! You .... for almost an hour! (talk)
   B Sorry! Here you are.
3. **A** Are you angry with me?
   B Yes, I am! I .... for you for an hour! (wait)
4. **A** You play the piano very well.
   B Thank you. I .... lessons for three years. (take)
5. **A** How long .... you .... English? (learn)
   B For about two years.
6. **A** .... you .... in this house for a long time? (live)
   B Yes – since I was born.

SB p. 119

9 Right or wrong? Put in a ✓ or ✗.

1 I have been knowing Henry for three years. ✓ ✗
2 We having been walking for hours and I'm tired. ✗
3 My sister's been annoying me all morning. ✓
4 We have been having our dog since last year. ✗
5 It's been snowing all day. It looks beautiful outside. ✓
6 They're not at home because they have been going on holiday. ✗
7 James has been playing the guitar since he was six. ✓
8 You have been getting the answer to question 3 wrong. ✗

10 Correct the wrong sentences.

1 I have known Henry for three haws.
2 We have been walking for hawes a. I'm tired
3 We have had our dog since last year.
4 They're not at home bec. they have gone...
5 You got the answer to question 3 wrong.

11 Complete with the present perfect simple or continuous form of the verbs in brackets.

Lisa Hi, Anna, it's me.

Anna What? From California?

Lisa Yeah, so let's keep it short. Tell everybody I'm fine.

Anna I will. Where exactly are you?

Lisa San Francisco.

Anna Oh. 1 Have you ~~been riding~~ ridden (ride) the cable cars?

Lisa Sure. And John and I 2 have ~~been~~ walked (walk) around a lot too. The others are just hanging out.

Anna Right. 3 Have you been (be) to any other places around San Francisco yet?

Lisa Well, we 4 have seen (see) some great places down south, and we're planning to go north to a national park tomorrow. We 5 have been having (have) a really good time.

Anna Good. Love to everybody. And Lisa?

Lisa Yeah?

Anna 6 Have you bought (buy) the California T-shirts I asked you about?

Lisa Not yet. I 7 have been looking (look), but I 8 haven't found (not find) them yet. But I will.

Anna OK, thanks. Love you.

Lisa Love you too. Bye.

Anna Bye.

SB p. 119

Vocabulary

12 Write the words under the pictures.

ridge backpack canyon dirt road

3 ridge

1 backpack 2 dirt road 4 canyon

13 Fill in the missing letters to make vocabulary items from the story about a holiday in Death Valley in your Student's Book on page 118.

1 d r y
2 s i g n a l
3 s p o t
4 c a n y o n
5 b a c k p a c k
6 r i d g e
7 h e a d q u a r t e r s
8 d i r t

14 Complete the dialogues with the words from 13.

1 **A** We're in trouble! Call your parents on your mobile phone.
B I can't! There's no signal here!

2 **A** Look at this photo. Do you know what this building is?
B Yes, it's the United Nations headquarters in New York.

3 **A** How do you carry things when you're cycling?
B I put everything in my backpack .

4 **A** Do you like cycling?
B Yes, but not in the city – I like to go to the mountains and cycle on dirt roads.

5 **A** I was at the match yesterday, too.
B I know – but there were so many people there, I couldn't spot you in the crowd.

6 **A** Why don't you wear your jeans?
B Because I washed them this morning and they aren't dry yet.

7 **A** We're going hiking across the Grand canyon this summer.
B Don't get too close to the edge of any ridge . I don't want you falling off!

SB p. 117

Developing speaking competencies

15 **Complete the dialogue with the questions in the box.**

a) How much is a return with a young person's railcard?
b) And one last thing. Can we get food on the train?
c) Sorry, just one more thing. What platform does the train leave from?
d) And what's the next one after that?
e) How long does it take to get there?
f) Excuse me, what time is the next train to Manchester?
g) Can we have two returns, please?

Pauline	1 ....
Assistant	Let me see. It's at 10.56.
Pauline	2 ....
Assistant	12.42.
Pauline	3 ....
Assistant	About an hour and a half. The 12.42 is a bit quicker because you don't need to change.
Pauline	4 ....
Assistant	It's £13.
Pauline	5 ....
Assistant	Certainly. That's £26.
Pauline	6 ....
Assistant	Yes, there is a buffet car.
Pauline	7 ....
Assistant	Eight, it's on the other side of the station.

CD4 17

16 **Listen and check your answers.**

Developing writing skills Asking for information

17 **CHOICES**

A **You weren't at school but you heard your class is planning a school picnic. Send your friend a text message (30–40 words).**

Ask him/her:

- where and when it is
- how you can get there
- if you should bring anything
- how long the picnic will be

SB p. 119, 120, 121

B Do the following tasks.

1 Read the task and what a student wrote. What does Caroline want to know about the ticket?

Task

You've been invited to a friend's holiday cottage*. You're sending her an email (40–70 words) to ask for some information.

In your email ask:

- about bus connections
- about getting a ticket
- if you have to bring something along

VOCABULARY
***cottage** – Hütte, Häuschen

From: caro13@mailconnect.com
Subject: Details please :)

REPLY

Hi Sarah,
Thank you for inviting me. I've already got the train ticket, but not the bus ticket to your village. Could you let me know how often there are buses and how long it takes? And do I get the ticket on the bus?
Should I bring my sleeping bag? Is there anything else I can bring with me?
Looking forward to seeing you.
Love,
Caroline

Useful language:

Asking for information

- How long does it take … ?
- How do I get to … ?
- How far is it … ?
- Is the walk … ?
- When does … leave?
- How much is a ticket?
- Can I book it online?
- Should I bring … ?
- Do you want me to … ?
- Do I have to change … at … ?

2 Now write your own answer to the following task.

Task

You've been invited to your aunt's new house in the mountains. You're sending her an email (40–70 words) to ask for some information.

In your email ask:

- where exactly her house is
- how you can get there
- what kind of clothes/shoes you should bring

SB p. 119

WORD FILE

A holiday in Death Valley

MORE Words and Phrases

1	**rent** sth	*They rented a car and drove around.*	etwas mieten
2	joking	*I'm only joking, of course.*	scherzen
	You bet!		Und ob! Aber sicher!
3	gold rush	*The California gold rush began in 1849.*	Goldrausch
	wine	*They make good wine in California, too.*	Wein
4	commute	*My parents' office is in another town. They have to commute.*	pendeln
	grocery store	*I'm going to the grocery store to buy some food.*	Lebensmittelladen
	seriously	*You seriously need to stop acting like a child – you're almost 18!*	wirklich, ernsthaft
6	gold digger	*Gold diggers were the people trying to find gold.*	Goldgräber/in
	spot	*Can you spot the animals over there?*	sehen; bemerken
	steep	*A canyon is a valley with steep sides of rock.*	steil
	thirst	*Some people died of thirst there. That's why it's called Death Valley.*	Durst
8a	crack	*My lips cracked because of the heat.*	aufspringen, rissig
	lips	*Her lips began to crack.*	Lippen
	shade	*I stayed in the shade of a giant rock.*	Schatten
	track	*There was a track through the mountains.*	Weg, Pfad
8b	four-wheel drive	*We need a jeep with four-wheel drive in the desert.*	mit Allradantrieb
	on top	*Soon we were on top of a ridge.*	oben; obenauf
	unbelievable	*That was an unbelievable adventure.*	unglaublich
13	made of	*The statue was made of gold.*	bestehend aus
ME1	get real	*Come on, get real!*	am Boden bleiben
	stay in	*The weather was bad, so we stayed in all day.*	zu Hause bleiben
DVD	**it takes ...**	*It takes about 9 hours to fly and 6 days by car.*	man braucht ...

Reading

1 **Read the newspaper article.**

A boating accident

Naseli and Lisa Nona were travelling on their boat from Badu Island to a birthday party on Thursday Island. With them were their four children, Stephen, 12, Norita, 10, Ellis, 15 and three-year-old Pete. After about one hour the motor of their boat stopped.

Naseli tried to repair it, but he couldn't. Then the weather became really bad. The heavy wind turned the boat over. The parents told Ellis, Norita and Stephen to swim to the nearest island.

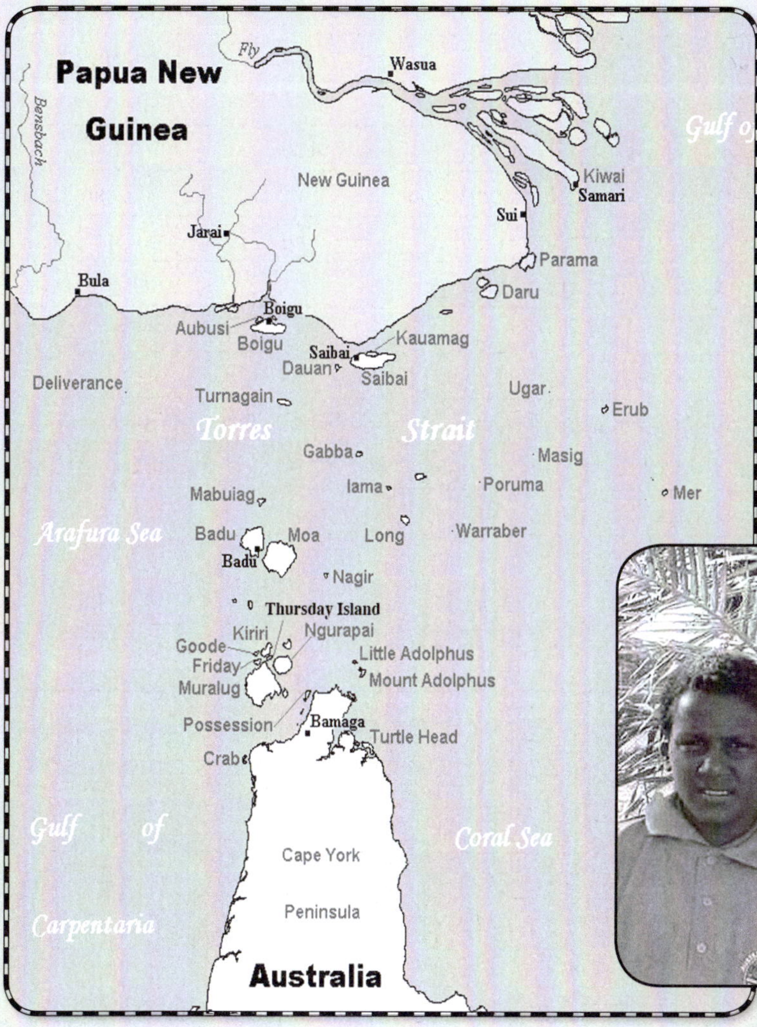

They were all good swimmers and swam for about three hours.

Finally they reached a little rock. They climbed onto the rock and hoped for a boat to come and rescue them. But nobody came. The children had to stay on the rock for two days and nights without water and food. Then Stephen and his sisters swam to another island. "I believe there's an island to the west. We must try to get there," Stephen said, "or we'll die!"

The children were lucky. When they reached the small island, they found plums and coconuts. Finally they were found on the island by their uncle after four days. Unfortunately, their parents and their little brother are still missing.

SB p. 124, 125

2 How many of these tasks can you do?

Complete the sentences with no more than 4 words.

1 The family was going to Thursday Island because there was a birthday party.
2 After some time there was a problem with the boate.
3 There was a strong wind. It turned the boad over.

4 The parents told
- ☒ all of their children to swim to the nearest island.
- ☐ their children to hold on to the boat.
- ☐ three of their children to swim to the nearest island.

5 The children on the rock were hoping
- ☒ for a boat to pass by.
- ☐ for the coastguard.
- ☐ for the helicopter rescue team.

6 The children left the rock
- ☐ on a boat.
- ☒ because the water was too high.
- ☐ because they needed drinking water.

7 How did they survive on the second island?
They had coconuts and plums to eat

8 How long did they stay on the second island?
They stayed on the second Island for two days

9 What happened to their parents do you think?
I think they died

3 Check your answers.

Listening

CD4 18

4 Listen to Sharon's story about an earthquake. Put the events into the correct order.

- ☐ They were relaxing at the hotel.
- ☐ Sharon crashed into her dad and her nose started to bleed.
- ☐ She was glad she didn't live in San Francisco.
- ☐ Suddenly the room began to shake.
- 1 An English girl, Sharon, and her family were staying in a hotel in San Francisco.
- ☐ Then the room shook again and they all ran to the doorway.
- ☐ She also said they should stand in a doorway* if there was another earthquake.
- ☐ Later she checked the internet and read that there were around 380 earthquakes a year.
- ☐ Then a painting fell on her ankle.
- ☐ The receptionist told them it was an earthquake.

VOCABULARY: ***stand in a doorway** – in einer Türe (in einem Türrahmen) stehen

SB p. 124, 125, 126

Essential Grammar The passive

5 Match the sentences and the pictures.

- [10] The baby woke us up.
- [5] The boy was hit by the football.
- [6] We made our teacher a cake.
- [2] The boy hit the football.
- [1] The man painted the woman.
- [8] The cat was chased by the dog.
- [7] The baby was woken up by a bird.
- [4] The man was painted by the woman.
- [9] The cat chased the dog.
- [3] The cake was made by our teacher.

6 Decide if the sentences are active or passive.

		Active	Passive
1	The hurricane destroyed thousands of homes.	X	
2	Breakfast is cooked by the chef.		X
3	He was paid a lot of money for the photo.		X
4	We're not very happy with our room.	X	
5	The teacher was ten minutes late for the lesson.	X	
6	The plane was full of people.		X
7	The bird ate the worm.	X	
8	The painting was stolen by thieves.		X
9	I wrote the poem.	X	
10	The race was won by Vettel.		X

SB p. 130

More Grammar The passive

7 **Complete the text with the correct form of the verbs in the present simple passive.**

Complete the entry card on the back and send it to us. Tell us why you think you could be a superstar.

All the cards 2 are read (read) by our jury*. 25 young people 3 are choosen (choose). They 4 are invited (invite) to our studio. They 5 are asked (ask) to show how fit they are in front of a camera. Their performance 6 are filmed (film). Then the films 7 are watched (watch) by the members of our jury. It's that easy. Send in this card – and you could become a new MEGASTAR! A week later, each of the final 10 young people 8 are asked (ask) to do some difficult tasks in front of a lot of people. Then the 3 winners 9 are chosen (choose) by these people – and the winner could be YOU!

VOCABULARY: *jury – Preisrichter

8 **Read the report by Mariangela Melata. Complete with past passive forms.** - 3 form

At three o'clock the people of Chiuso 1 were woken (wake) by an earthquake. I 2 was thrown (throw) out of my bed and in a few minutes most of my apartment 3 was destroyed (destroy). I ran out into the streets. Many of the buildings around me 4 were damaged (damage) and most of the windows 5 were broken (break). The main street 6 was blocked (block) by two fallen trees. During the day all the shops 7 were closed (close).

9 **Read the text. Choose verbs from the box and use them in the past passive form to complete the text.**

damage	treat
injure	~~kill~~
close	destroy
take	

In yesterday's avalanche two people 1 were killed and eight 2 were injure and 3 were taken to hospital. They 4 were treaten for shock and some cuts. One ski lift 5 was damaged and a small cottage 6 was completely destroyed. The ski lifts 7 were closed for the rest of the day.

SB p. 130

Vocabulary

10 **Find the nine words for natural disasters. (→ ← ↘)**

I	E	R	I	F	T	S	E	R	O	F	T	S	U	N	A	M	I	I
Q	D	T	C	L	L	P	Y	B	H	A	Z	M	T	V	I	O	L	G
A	T	I	F	F	C	O	R	H	Z	A	P	C	H	D	I	W	H	Q
D	R	O	U	G	H	T	O	S	E	A	R	T	H	Q	U	A	K	E
E	D	I	L	S	D	U	M	D	G	T	Q	S	L	Y	Y	H	L	Q
N	O	I	T	P	U	R	E	C	I	N	A	C	L	O	V	K	I	F
H	U	R	R	I	C	A	N	E	E	H	C	N	A	L	A	V	A	H

11 **Use the words from 10 to write under the pictures.**

1 an earthquake

2 a flood

3 a forest fire

4 an avalanche

5 a drought

6 a mudslide

7 a volcanic eruption

8 a hurricane

12 **Write *away* / *under* / *near* in each sentence.**

1 Don't stand ...near... a tree if there's a storm.
2 Keep ...away... from a volcano if it's going to erupt.
3 During a tsunami, buildings ...under... the coast are in great danger.
4 If there's an earthquake, it's a good idea to lie ...under... a desk or table.
5 There was a mudslide ...near... the village.
6 During a flood, keep ...away... from electricity.

13 **Read the text. Complete with the words in the box. There is one extra word.**

collapsed cracks crushed died escaped rescue safe earthquake

There was a terrible [1]...earthquake... last night in Japan. It measured 7.2 on the Richter scale. Some streets in the cities have big [2]........................ in them. Many older houses [3]........................ and some people inside them were [4]........................ . Some people were lucky – they [5]........................ and now they are [6]........................ . Workers are trying to find people who are still alive and [7]........................ them.

SB p. 124, 126

14 CHOICES

A **Write a short story (40–70 words) about a car accident you saw.**

Write about:

- where it was
- why the accident happened
- what happened to the drivers (was anybody hurt?)
- what happened to the cars (damage)

B **Do the following tasks.**

1 Read the task and what a student wrote. What was the climber's mistake?

Task

Imagine you got caught in an avalanche. Write the story of what happened (120–150 words).

In your story say:

- where you were and who was with you
- why the avalanche happened
- how it affected you
- how you were rescued
- what happened afterwards

There were four of us, and we climbed the Matterhorn up the 'normal route', past the 'Hörnligrat'. We were all good climbers and the sun shone so we thought it would be no problem. When we were up at around 4,000 metres we took a quick rest. I put my rucksack down but I made the mistake of putting it too far away from me and it started sliding down. I tried to grab the bag and suddenly I slid down too. I only stopped after about a hundred metres but everything seemed OK.

As I tried to climb back up, the snow broke away under me and it started an avalanche. It was not a big one, but it carried me away and soon I was under the snow – how deep, I didn't know. There was a small pocket of air next to my face, and I was able to shout, but nobody heard me. I breathed hard and I felt very dizzy.

After what seemed an eternity* a hand reached down to my face, and a few minutes later my friends dug me out of the snow. It turned out my right arm was broken. That was the end of my Matterhorn dream.

VOCABULARY: *eternity – Ewigkeit

SB p. 130

Language tip: Narrative tenses (1)

We usually use past forms to tell stories. We use past simple to describe most of the action but don't forget to use the past continuous to:

- set the scene
- describe an action happening at a certain time
- describe a longer action that is interrupted by a short action

2 There are six cases in the text where the past continuous would be better. Replace the past simple forms with the past continuous ones.

was breathing was shining was sliding was trying were climbing were digging

Writing tip:

Writing a story (2) – Adding drama

- Try and use dramatic vocabulary, for example: *grab* (not *hold*), *huge* or *enormous* (not *very big*).
- Use repetitions (He hoped that ... And he hoped that ... And he also hoped that ...).
- Check your story develops in a logical way.
- If possible put in something unexpected/surprising/dramatic ... .
- Use good introductory words to your sentences. Do not only use *and, but, also*.

3 Now write your own answer to the following task.

Task

Imagine you had an accident on a boat. Write a story about it.
In your story say:

- where you were and who was with you
- why the accident happened
- what happened to you / the others
- how you were rescued
- what happened afterwards

Everyday English The phone call

DVD Look at the phrases on p. 131 in your Student's Book again. Use them to complete the dialogues.

1 A I think I need to buy a new mobile.
B .... But if I were you, I'd just buy a new battery.

2 A I think it's going to rain. Can I borrow your umbrella, please? ....
B Sure! ....
A Thanks.

3 A Somebody told Chris that I took Lisa to the cinema yesterday!
B Hey! .... I didn't tell him.

SB p. 130, 131

WORD FILE

Natural disasters

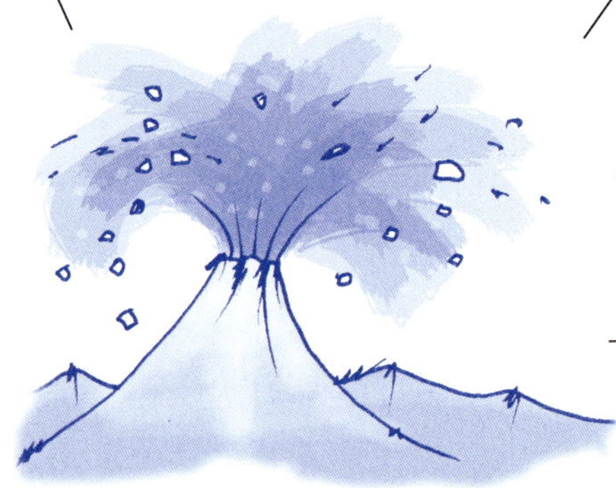

MORE Words and Phrases

1	**disaster**	*The tsunami in 2004 was a great disaster of the modern world.*	Katastrophe, Unglück
2a	be trapped	*Two children were trapped in a building.*	eingeschlossen sein
	collapse	*A woman was trapped under her collapsed home.*	zusammenbrechen, einstürzen
	measure	*The earthquake measured 6.6 on the Richter scale.*	(ab)messen
	(rescue) operation	*The international rescue operation saved a lot of people.*	Rettungseinsatz
	survive	*I don't know how we survived the bus ride.*	überleben
	survivor	*After the rescue operation only a few survivors were found.*	Überlebende/r
2b	ash	*The volcano sent ash and rocks into the air.*	Asche
	erupt	*The volcano erupted on June 3rd.*	ausbrechen
	evacuate	*60,000 people were evacuated from the island.*	evakuieren, räumen
	luckily	*Luckily, the evacuation saved thousands of lives.*	glücklicherweise
	undersea	*A huge undersea earthquake happened in the Indian Ocean.*	Unterwasser-; unter Wasser
	warn	*Scientists warned about the danger.*	warnen
3	**injured**	*Many people were injured.*	verletzt
	keep away from	*Keep away from trees in a storm.*	fernbleiben von
4	crush	*The car had been crushed under a tree.*	zusammendrücken; zerquetschen
	underneath	*Get underneath the kitchen table in an earthquake.*	unter
5	raft	*Chuck built a raft to escape from the island.*	Floß
	turn into	*The rainfall quickly turned into heavy snowfall.*	werden zu, sich verwandeln in
8	**choice**	*You can choose a record or a book. It's your choice.*	Wahl
	pleasure	*It's a pleasure to be here.*	Freude, Vergnügen
	plenty	*I'll have plenty of time to learn all of it.*	genügend, jede Menge
10	**advice**	*I don't know what to do. Can you give me some advice?*	Ratschlag
	desert island	*How do you survive when you are a castaway on a desert island?*	einsame Insel
	moving	*It was a sad story and very moving.*	bewegend, ergreifend
11	**burn**	*The forest was burning.*	(ver-)brennen
	in case …	*I'll tell you again tomorrow in case you forget.*	für den Fall, dass …, falls
ME1	**shall**	*Shall I get you a cup of tea and an aspirin?*	sollen
	the oldest trick in the book	*This is the oldest trick in the book, Harry.*	der älteste Trick, den es gibt

UNIT 13 Dilemmas

Reading

1 Read the story. Put the pictures in the correct order.

A dilemma

D

A

C

E

B

F

I went to the cinema yesterday. I saw John outside. He's Sandra's boyfriend, and Sandra is my best friend. I could see that he was a bit nervous. "I'm sure he is nervous because Sandra is not here yet," I thought.

Anyway, suddenly this girl came over. She took John by the hand and said, "Come on, John, the film's going to start in a minute." And off they went. He didn't even say goodbye to me. I was shocked. I didn't want to see the film any more. I went home.

When I got home, the phone rang. It was Sandra. "We couldn't go out," she said. "John had so much homework for English and I had to do my Maths homework."

"Should I tell her about John and that other girl?" I thought to myself. Sandra just said, "Bye Jenny!" and she hung up. I couldn't sleep that night. I was feeling so bad. I didn't know what to do. What a dilemma!

The next day, after school, I saw Sandra and John in the street. They were fighting and shouting loudly. I was shocked.

Then Sandra saw me. She was really angry. "You knew about this!" she shouted at me. "You knew! You saw him at the cinema, didn't you?"

Then John came over and said, "Sandra, it's not Jenny's fault – shout at me, not at her!" But Sandra just looked at me and said, "I hate you! I hate both of you!" And then she walked away.

Sandra still doesn't speak to me. I never see John any more. So I've lost two friends and I don't know why.

SB p. 134, 135

2 How many of these tasks can you do?

Complete the sentences with no more than 4 words.

1 John and Jenny are ....
2 Jenny thought John was waiting ....
3 Jenny was .... that she didn't go into the cinema.

4 Jenny didn't know John was at the cinema. T / F
5 Jenny was angry when she put the phone down. T / F
6 Jenny was kept awake by the dilemma. T / F

7 Why was Sandra so angry with Jenny?

....

8 How did John react when Sandra shouted at Jenny?

....

9 Do you think Jenny did the right thing? Why (not)?

....

3 Check your answers.

Listening

CD4 19

4 Listen to Eve and Ken playing the dilemma game. Put the situations in the order that you hear them.

A

B

C

CD4 19

5 Listen again and answer the questions with *Eve* or *Ken*.

Who would ...

1 want to know where their brother spent the night? ....
2 do what their brother wanted them to do? ....
3 refuse to tell the teacher all they knew? ....
4 say nothing about the window if they were the guilty person? ....
5 leave the wallet on the floor? ....
6 try and find out who the wallet belonged to? ....

6 Now write your answer to each dilemma from 4.

Dilemma A ....
Dilemma B ....
Dilemma C ....

SB p. 134, 135

Essential Grammar 2nd Conditional

7 Match the beginnings and endings of the sentences.

1 If I had enough money,	☐ you'd get better marks.
2 If my brother had a problem,	☐ I'd buy a new computer.
3 If I found some money in the street,	☐ would you tell me?
4 If you worked harder,	☐ I'd take it to the police station.
5 If I was president of Austria,	☐ I'd change lots of things.
6 If you knew the answer,	☐ I'd help him.

8 Put the dialogue in the correct order.

[1] **A** I'd like to get better marks at school.
☐ **A** That's right. And then I'd lose marks for being late.
☐ **A** Well, if I got tired, I'd need to sleep more.
☐ **A** Yeah, but if I studied more, I'd get tired in the evening.
☐ **B** What's the problem with being tired?
☐ **B** Well, if you studied more, you'd get better marks.
[8] **B** Oh dear. My head hurts!
☐ **B** And if you slept more, you wouldn't wake up in time for school.

9 Read the sentences and tick the correct boxes.

1 If my father was here, I would be happy.
I am happy. yes ☐ no ☐

2 If Polly didn't live in London, I would see her more often.
Polly lives in London. yes ☐ no ☐

3 If I had a dictionary, I would look this word up.
I know the meaning of this word. yes ☐ no ☐

4 If my computer wasn't broken, I would write some emails.
I'm writing emails. yes ☐ no ☐

5 If your mother was here, she wouldn't let you do that!
Your mother is not here. yes ☐ no ☐

6 The teacher would be angry if she knew.
The teacher knows. yes ☐ no ☐

10 Circle the correct word.

1 If I *have* / *had* more money, I'd buy it for you.
2 If you *go* / *went* to London, you'd learn a lot of English.
3 If it was my birthday today, *I'd get* / *I got* a lot of presents.
4 I would help you if I *didn't* / *wouldn't* have homework to do.
5 If he *would have* / *had* a girlfriend, he'd be very happy.
6 If there was a test tomorrow, I *wouldn't* / *didn't* pass.
7 What *did* / *would* you do if you found money in the street?
8 He *didn't* / *wouldn't* like New York if he lived there.

SB p. 137

More Grammar 2nd Conditional

11 Write the sentences.

1 I don't like Sally. I don't talk to her.
If I liked Sally, I'd talk to her.

2 He doesn't have a computer. I don't send him emails.
If

3 She's ill. She isn't at school.
If

4 I like you. I help you with your homework.
If

5 They're on holiday. They aren't here today.
If

6 My modem is broken. I don't surf the internet.
If

12 Look at the pictures. Write three more dialogues.

lose your key

see a famous person

see your teacher at the school disco

be headmaster of your school

1 A What would you do if you lost your key?
B I'd go to my friend's house.

2 A
B

3 A
B

4 A
B

13 Write your own answer to the questions.

1 What would you do if your best friend stopped talking to you?

2 What would you do if you lost your wallet?

3 What would you do if you won a lot of money?

4 What would you do if you were the president of your country?

5 What would you do if you could travel in time?

6 What would you do if you forgot who you were?

SB p. 137

Vocabulary

14 **Find eight words in the word snake.**

picksnerdgroupcheekygroundeddetentionweirddilemma

15 **Complete each sentence with one of the words from 14.**

1 My parents got angry with me and they've .... me for a week!
2 He often gets into trouble for saying .... things to the teacher.
3 I don't know what the right thing to do is. It's a real .... for me.
4 He shouldn't wear those silly glasses – he looks like a .... with them.
5 If you talk in class, you'll get ....
6 He's a real bully* – he always .... on smaller kids.
7 Look at his clothes! They're all green! That's really .... !
8 I'm going out on Friday with a .... of kids from school.

VOCABULARY: ***bully** – jemand, der andere tyrannisiert

16 **Complete the mini-dialogues with the words in the box. There are two extra words.**

ask me out	trouble	lonely	deserve	stay behind
rude	by mistake	meet up	lent	owe me

1 **Anthony** Hey, why did you open my letter?
Mum Sorry, I opened it ....

2 **Julian** Nina is much too nice for you – you don't .... her.
David If you say that again, you're in ....

3 **Sophie** Do you think Jim will .... with us this weekend?
Karen I'm not sure, he said he wanted to .... with his friends.

4 **Fred** You still .... the money I gave you for the book.
Adrian Sorry, I completely forgot you .... it to me.

5 **John** Why did Amy say that to me? It was really unkind.
Sara Don't worry too much about it. Sometimes she can be really ....

17 **Now write three mini-dialogues with the words from the box in your exercise book.**

SB p. 134, 135

Developing writing skills Poem

18 CHOICES

A Write a short poem about your school day.

Remember: It doesn't have to rhyme. It can be serious or funny.

B Do the following tasks.

1 Read the task and what a student wrote. What is the Butterfly Lady's wish for herself?

Task **You were asked to contribute an IF-poem to a poetry website. Write a poem. Think about:**

- a situation / a person / an incident for your poem
- a way to repeat the *if*-construction
- a punchline
- a title

The Butterfly Lady

If I could have three wishes
I'd wish for another three
But I know that in all fairy tales
This is something that cannot be.
So if I had three wishes
I'd wish for a peaceful world
In which nobody has to go hungry
In which nobody is without home.

But for me I would wish for twelve butterflies
That fly around or behind me
So wherever I go
People would know
Here comes the butterfly lady
Who makes them smile
At least for a while.

Language tip:

Writing poetry

When writing a poem always think carefully about the language.

- Which word is the best?
- Which words or phrases should I repeat?
- Should I use rhyming words or not?
- How long are the lines of my poem?
- Think of a strong opening line to attract the reader's attention.

SB p. 137

2 Read the text again and find out:

- how many *if*-sentences there are
- how many rhymes there are
- how many repetitions there are

Writing tip:

Writing a poem

There are many ways to write a poem. Here are some things to consider:

- Think of what you want to write about (e.g. the seasons, a person, an animal).
- Think of how long your poem should be (e.g. is it a one-stanza poem?).
- Think about rhyming words – a poem doesn't have to rhyme!
- If you want to rhyme, there are some good rhyming dictionaries online.

The most important thing is:
Just write. And write. And write.
And then rewrite and rewrite.
Ask a friend for feedback. And rewrite and rewrite.

3 Now write your own answer to the following task.

Task

You were asked to contribute a poem about summer to a poetry website. Write the poem. Think about:

- what aspect of summer you want to write about
- if it's a nature poem or a people poem
- whether you want to use rhymes
- a good title for your poem

MORE Words and Phrases

	dilemma	*She's in a real dilemma.*	Dilemma, Zwangslage
1	**give sb an alibi**	*Would you give your brother an alibi if he came home too late?*	jdm ein Alibi verschaffen
2	ID (= identification)	*Do you have any ID with you?*	Ausweis
	tell on sb	*Tina told on her friend.*	jdn vertratschen/verpetzen
3	(get/have) detention	*I had to stay late after school because I got detention.*	nachsitzen müssen
5	coach	*The coach doesn't want me to be on the football team.*	Trainer/in
	owe sb sth	*He owed his brother a lot of money.*	jdm etwas schulden
6	nerd	*He's not very popular with the other kids. He's a bit of a nerd.*	Streber/in, Sonderling
	outsider	*No one really likes me here. I feel like such an outsider!*	Außenstehende/r; Außenseiter/in
G	**get to know** sb	*She got to know his friends at the party.*	jdn kennenlernen
	pick on sb	*I don't like her. She picks on you all the time.*	auf jdm herumhacken
ME1	roar	*The roar of a waterfall is nice.*	hier: das Rauschen

SB p. 137

Reading

1 Read the text about a tour to the Okavango Delta in Botswana.

Classic Botswana

What is the Okavango Delta?

It is one of the world's most famous wilderness areas. The delta is formed by thousands of channels* of the Okavango River with clear water. There are a lot of small islands and larger dry open areas with bush and a lot of trees. The Okavango is home to more than 400 different kinds of birds and large herds* of buffalo, antelopes* and elephants. You will also find crocodiles, hippos, cheetahs*, leopards, lions and different kinds of monkeys. In July and August, during Botswana's dry winter months, the delta swells to three times its size. That makes the area one with Africa's greatest concentration of wildlife.

VOCABULARY: ***channels** – Kanäle; **herd** – Herde; **antelope** – Antilope; **cheetah** – Gepard; **spotlight** – Suchscheinwerfer

What are the camps like?

There are camps with stone bungalows or very nice tents, each with a private shower and toilet. In each camp there is also a large dining room where all meals are taken by the guests, and a shop where you can buy souvenirs. Of course, there are also luxury camps with private balconies and very large rooms. Many camps offer great views of the country, and you can enjoy waking to the sounds of wildlife. Normally, people go to at least one water camp and one bush camp.

What can you do at the camp?

You get up at six o'clock and have a wonderful breakfast. Then at half past six the first drive of the day starts, and it ends at ten or eleven. When you stay in a camp in one of the large dry areas you will go for a drive in a Land Rover.

When you stay in a water camp you will either go by boat or by canoe which is called a 'mokoro'. There are only seats for two people in a mokoro. The guide uses a long stick to push the canoe along.

When you come back to the camp, lunch will be waiting for you. Then you can rest or relax until five. At five there is the second drive of the day and part of it will be in the dark. The guides will use a spotlight* to look for animals.

When you come back at about nine, dinner will be waiting for you. After that, you may have a chat round the camp fire.

When you go to bed, a guide will go with you to your bungalow or tent as there may be wild animals like elephants or lions around.

SB p. 140–143

2 How many of these tasks can you do?

Complete the sentences with no more than 4 words.

1 Thousands of channels from the Okavango River ....

2 More than 400 birds ....

3 The delta is three times bigger in ....

4 Bungalows and tents

☐ all have private showers and toilets. ☐ all have a kitchen.

☐ are often very uncomfortable.

5 In each camp

☐ you can cook your meal yourself.

☐ there is a large dining room where you can take your meals.

☐ there is a dining room for dinner only.

6 Most people

☐ wake up early in the camps. ☐ stay in two different types of camps.

☐ stay in luxury camps.

7 What do guests do in the morning?

....

8 What do guests do in the afternoon?

....

9 What do guests do in the early evening?

....

3 Check your answers.

Listening

CD4 20

4 Listen to Larissa talking about Mma Ramotswe. Then answer the questions below.

1 What are the two favourite hobbies of Larissa's family?

....

2 How many books has Alexander McCall Smith written so far about Mma Ramotswe?

....

3 Who is Mma Ramotswe?

....

4 What kind of character is she?

....

5 What does Mma Ramotswe teach us about Africa?

....

6 Why does Larissa think that McCall Smith is good at writing about Africa?

....

SB p. 140–143

Essential Grammar *going to*

5 Read what the kids say. Then write the names under the pictures.

Jonathan: I'm going to work in a restaurant.
George: I'm going to write successful books.
Maria: I'm going to be a French teacher.
Miriam: I'm going to open a shop.
Sid: I'm going to marry Maria.
Mike: I'm going to run in the London Marathon.
Hannah: I'm going to win a lot of money.
Anna: I'm going to design furniture.

1 .... 2 .... 3 .... 4 ....

5 .... 6 .... 7 .... 8 ....

6 Read the poem and complete with the *going to* forms.

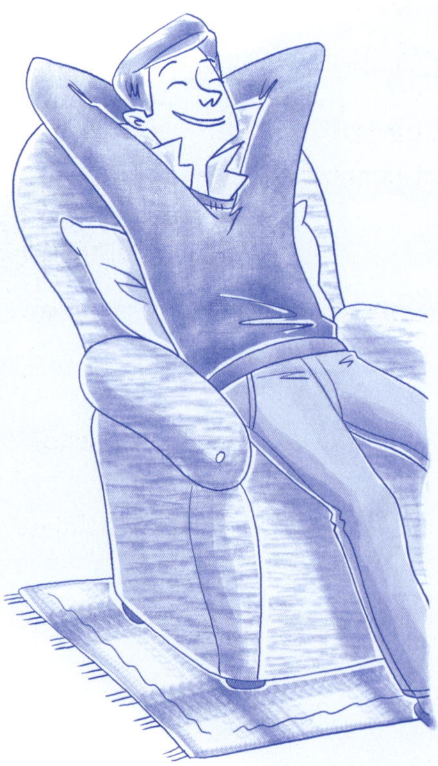

I [1].. (get) on a plane
And fly away
I [2].. (find) a country
Where I want to stay
I [3].. (find) a job there
And buy a welcome mat
I [4].. (earn) a lot of money
And buy a flat
I [5].. (put) the mat
In front of the door
I [6].. (wait) and wait
And sit on the floor
One day I [7].. (hear) a knock
And there's a lovely girl outside
We [8].. (fall) in love and then
A year after that she'll be my bride.

And NOW I [9].. (wake)
From my dreams
I [10].. (make) some tea ...
Yeah, and a good idea it seems.

SB p. 146

More Grammar *going to*

7 **Complete with the correct form of *going to* and the verbs in brackets.**

From: val14@mailconnect.com
Subject: Our holiday this year ☺

REPLY

Hi Marleen,
We've planned our holiday – I think. We [1] .... (drive) around Scotland, since you've never been there. We [2] .... (see) as many places as possible. We [3] .... (not go) camping this year. We [4] .... (stay) in small hotels.
Dad [5] .... (rent) a car, unless he forgets. Don't worry – I [6] .... (remind) him right away.
Best,
Valerie

8 **Complete the email with the correct form of *going to* and the words in the box.**

fly
meet
take
stay
be
use
go

From: alex.s@mailconnect.com
Subject: Holiday plans!

Hi Tim,
Guess what! We [1] .... to Botswana in July because that is when you can see a lot of animals.
First we [2] .... to Gaborone. Dad [3] .... some people there and then we [4] .... in the Okavango Delta for a few days. Of course, I [5] .... a lot of pictures, and I [6] .... them for a slide show at school.
I'm sure it [7] .... awfully interesting.
Alex

9 **Complete the questions.**

1 A What ....are you going to do.......... at the weekend?
B I'm going to do nothing!
2 A What .... do in the holidays?
B I'm going to stay home for three weeks.
3 A Who .... organise the party?
B My friends are going to help me.
4 A Why .... play football today?
B Because my leg hurts.
5 A What .... do when you leave school?
B I'm going to work in a bank.

SB p. 146

Vocabulary

10 Choose the correct answers.

1	2	3	4	5	6	7
a) planned	a) checked	a) done	a) found	a) look	a) buy	a) buy
b) found	b) hired	b) made	b) looked	b) surf	b) watch	b) hire
c) looked	c) made	c) had	c) asked	c) check	c) look	c) make

A Have you [1]................................... your trip yet?

B Most of it. My dad's [2]................................... a car to drive us to the airport and we've [3]................................... the hotel reservation.

A What are you going to do there?

B I'm not sure. We haven't [4]................................... out about all the things there are to do.

A Why don't you [5]................................... out the area on the internet?

B That's not a bad idea. Maybe I can [6]................................... at a map of the area online.

A What about the language? Are you taking lessons?

B No. I think I'll [7]................................... a dictionary to use there.

A Well good luck, and don't forget to send me a postcard.

B I won't!

11 Tick the verbs and phrases that go together.

	a holiday	a trip	a hotel reservation	a car	a dictionary	a map of the area	the area out on the web	out about good restaurants	information about the best beaches
find									
book									
make									
plan									
buy				✓					
hire				✓					
check									

12 Match the words and the definitions.

1 wilderness
2 check out something
3 attach
4 ranger
5 die out
6 official

☐ to fasten one thing to another
☐ not exist any longer
☐ wild and natural area where only few people live
☐ a person with responsibility in an organisation
☐ to find out if something is true
☐ a person whose job it is to protect a national park

SB p. 144, 145

Developing writing skills Summary

13 CHOICES

A **Choose a story from your Student's Book or Workbook and write a summary (80–100 words). Do not tell too many details and use present tense for your summary.**

B **Do the following tasks.**

1 Read the task and what a student wrote. Why are Alessia and George worried?

Task

Your teacher asked you to write a summary of the story *Alessia* (Student's Book, p. 74; 140–170 words).

Write about:

- who Alessia is
- what George thinks about her
- what his mum wants him to do
- how he reacts
- how George and Alessia slowly become friends
- what their problem is

"Alessia" is about a girl who comes to England from a foreign country and who can't speak English. The boy next door is a bit disappointed because he was hoping for a boy he could play football with.

Soon after Alessia and her parents move in, George's mother asks him to take things to her like old books and games. George doesn't like this, and suddenly thinks he needs all these things himself.

But George's mother insists, and George actually likes the way Alessia smiles at him when George goes there.

George goes to see Alessia more and more often, and after a while George quite likes Alessia. Alessia's English has improved and George often talks to Alessia. George even steps in when someone is bullying Alessia at school.

Two years later George and Alessia are good friends. Unfortunately, Alessia's parents are talking about moving, and George and Alessia are rather unhappy about this.

Language tip:

Using pronouns

Pronouns are useful because they help you avoid repetition of nouns in your writing. However, it is important to use the correct ones and make sure it's clear what they refer to. Otherwise you can easily confuse your reader.

SB p. 144

2 Read the text again. In the first two paragraphs 6 pronouns have been highlighted.

a) What do they refer to?

In the rest of the text no pronouns have been used for George and Alessia.

b) How could you replace the names with pronouns? Be careful not to replace them all.

Writing tip:

Writing a summary

- Read the text carefully and underline the most important information.
- Make sure you don't mention too many details.
- Use the present tense for your summary.
- Use time expressions (*soon after, after a while, two years later …*).
- Connect ideas (*and, but, because, actually …*).
- Avoid direct speech in your summary.
- Think carefully how to use paragraphs.
- Stick to the number of words for your summary.

3 Now write your own answer to the following task.

Task

Your teacher asked you to write a summary of the story *Going to Granada* on p. 20 in your Workbook (140–170 words).
Write about:

- who is going to Granada
- why they are going there
- what happens after the plane lands
- what happens on the van
- how they get off the van

Everyday English Red kite alert

DVD Look at the phrases on p. 147 in your Student's Book again. Use them to complete the dialogues.

1 A Let's ask Mum if we can stay out late tonight.
B Why? She'll say no for sure. It's …………………………………… .

2 A Hey you guys. Come with me to the cinema tonight.
B Sorry, no – we're all busy.
A Oh, all right. I'll go …………………………………… then.

3 A That new boy in class is awful. He's always talking and making trouble.
…………………………………… . I can't stand him!
B You're …………………………………… . I don't like him either – no one does really.

SB p. 144, 147

MORE Words and Phrases

	wilderness	*Go into the heart of the wilderness.*	Wildnis
1	**check out** sth	*Check out where the capital is.*	etwas untersuchen, überprüfen
	dimwit	*Don't be a dimwit. Be clever!*	Dummkopf, Hohlkopf
	official	*The official language is English.*	offiziell, amtlich
3	**attach**	*I've attached the MP3-file to my email.*	anhängen
	phone call	*The man on the balcony was making a phone call.*	Anruf
	wetland	*The Okavango Delta is a large wetland.*	Sumpfgebiet
5	die out	*Leopards might die out.*	aussterben
	imitation	*Don't worry, it's just an imitation, it's not real fur.*	Nachahmung; Fälschung
	leopard	*A leopard is a large wild cat.*	Leopard
	otherwise	*We need to protect them. Otherwise they'll die out.*	andernfalls, sonst
	skin	*Selling leopard skins is illegal.*	Haut; hier: Fell
6	hyena	*Hyenas try to get leopards' food.*	Hyäne
	lodge	*Outside in the wilderness we lived in a lodge.*	Hütte; hier: Lager
8	ranger	*The ranger will show you around the park.*	Aufseher/in; Ranger/in
	turn over	*The car turned over and landed on its roof.*	(sich) umdrehen; hier: überschlagen
11	accommodation	*It's easy to find good accommodation in this area.*	Unterkunft; Unterbringung
	preparation	*The producer controls the preparation of a film.*	Vorbereitung
G	sunburned	*She's going to get sunburned!*	Sonnenbrand haben
ME1	show-off	*You're such a show-off!*	Angeber/in
ME3	scuba diving	*I'm planning to learn scuba diving this summer.*	(Sport-)Tauchen
	wildlife	*We're going to see the wildlife on our trip to Botswana.*	wilde Natur

Answer key – Workbook

Name:

Class:

UNIT 1

❷ 1 T, 2 T, 3 F
4 do a charity concert to raise money for computers. 5 discuss it with the band. 6 did not all agree with Josh.
7 He thinks that charity is about people and not about computers.
8 They will give half of the money to a children's home. 9 There were not enough tickets for the first one. / The room wasn't big enough for all the people.

❹ 1 also in some lessons at school. 2 pop. 3 on Spotify. 4 two instruments. 5 the guitar. 6 music by Bob Dylan and Janis Joplin.
7 listening to classical music.
8 a CD player.

❺ 1 play, 2 sings, 3 plays, 4 sing, 5 play, 6 do, 7 writes, 8 write, 9 don't, 10 doesn't

❻ 1 dreamt, 2 got, 3 didn't know, 4 took, 5 practised, 6 didn't want, 7 wanted, 8 studied, 9 didn't think, 10 fell, 11 said, 12 could, 13 couldn't, 14 had, 15 went, 16 talked, 17 asked, 18 loved, 19 agreed

❼ **1** 1 What's your favourite band, Nigel? 2 What do you like about Maroon 5? 3 And what do you like about *Little Mix?*
2 1 Do you like dancing, Janice? 2 When did you start dancing? 3 Do you have a favourite band to dance to?
3 1 Do you listen to a lot of music, Henry? 2 And where do you get your music from? 3 Did you ever buy CDs?

❾ 1 audition, 2 give up, 3 takes, 4 give, 5 make, 6 training, 7 way, 8 get

❿ 1 take place, 2 raise, 3 donation, 4 performing, 5 famous, 6 lyrics

⓫ 1 d), 2 c), 3 g), a) 4 f), b)

⓭ B **1** He didn't like the way it had so much piano in it.

UNIT 2

❶ A lucky coincidence

❷ 1 F, 2 F, 3 T
4 a nice man, 5 tried to hide so, 6 for lunch
7 He was walking through a wood. 8 He drove them home. 9 He didn't say a bad word about him any more.

❺ Sarah

❻ 1 watching, 2 started, 3 having, 4 working, 5 fell, 6 rang, 7 reading

❼ 3, 9, 7, 8, 6, 2, 10, 5, 4, 1

❾ 1 was walking, 2 saw, 3 opened, 4 found, 5 was thinking, 6 saw, 7 was shopping, 8 didn't look, 9 asked, 10 knew

❿ 1 Dawn broke her leg when she was playing football.
2 Henry was drinking coffee when he dropped his cup. / Henry dropped his cup when he was drinking coffee.
3 June was walking the dog when it started raining.
4 Pip was working at the computer when his chair broke. / Pip broke his chair when he was working at the computer. / Pip's chair broke when he was working at the computer.
5 Miriam was reading a book when her headache started. / Miriam's headache started when she was reading a book.
6 Billy was listening to his MP3-player when he crashed into a lamp post. / Billy crashed into a lamp post when he was listening to his MP3-player. 7 Sue fell asleep when the teacher was talking. 8 Richard was eating an apple when his tooth fell out. / Richard's tooth fell out when he was eating an apple.

⓫ 1 MP3-player, CD, 2 mobile phone, 3 cap, sunglasses, 4 bill

⓬ 1 pay the bill, 2 tried the sunglasses on, 3 listening to his MP3-player, 4 talking on her mobile phone, 5 listen to CDs, 6 try on a cap

⓭ 1 cross, 2 try on, 3 similar, 4 tune, 5 decide, 6 survive, 7 handbag, 8 incredible, 9 enter, 10 fictional, 11 huge

⓮ B **1** two

Everyday English
1 That's not fair, 2 watch out, 3 Serves you right, 4 I know what you mean

UNIT 3

❷ 1 Lucille's mother, 2 Granada/Nicaragua, 3 a bus to Granada
4 it was very different to bus stations in the UK. 5 but the driver drove really fast. 6 was full of people.

❹ 1 Jeremy → William, 2 book → movie/film, 3 sofa → carpet, 4 quick → lovely long, 5 angry → happy

❺ 1. Spalte: 3, 1, 2   2. Spalte: 5, 6, 4

❻ 1 While, 2 During, 3 during, 4 While, 5 during, 6 during, 7 while, 8 While

❼ 1 When, before, until, By the time, 2 After, During, While, 3 before/after/during, While, When, 4 During, until, Before, When

❾ 1 has taken, 2 took, 3 takes, 4 will take

❿ 1 get, 2 met, 3 hired, 4 slept, 5 went, 6 suffered, 7 got, 8 took

⓫ 5, 4, 1, 6, 7, 2, 3

⓬ 1 sets off, 2 gets on, 3 gets to, 4 takes/gets on, 5 takes, 6 gets off, 7 takes, 8 gets to

⓭ 1 going, 2 should, 3 got, 4 say, 5 forget, 6 correct, 7 recommend, 8 that's

⓯ B **1** Because Tony should book soon.

UNIT 4

❶ 1 box jellyfish, 2 tiger snake, 3 redback spider, 4 stonefish, 5 saltwater crocodile

❷ 1 seven metres long, 2 on the northeastern coast / in the

northeast, 3 to hold your arm
4 T, 5 F, 6 T, 7 Because it's only 2.5 cm long and very difficult to see in the water. 8 You have two hours. 9 You should take care and read the signs.

4 Ryan – white dog, Helen – snake, Steve – tarantula

5 1 a spider or a lizard, 2 It's quite small and it's got long fur. 3 a cat and a dog, 4 friendly, 5 His mother said they were too much work and Steve was too lazy to look after a pet properly. 6 huge, hairy, poisonous, aggressive, ugly

6 1 F, 2 F, 3 T, 4 F, 5 F, 6 T, 7 T, 8 T, 9 F, 10 F

7 1 good, 2 an awesome, 3 worst, 4 most exciting, 5 boring, 6 better, 7 funnier, 8 more interesting, 9 great, 10 more, 11 funny, 12 greatest

8 1 the best, 2 the cutest, 3 the prettiest, 4 the coolest, 5 the most intelligent, 6 the most expensive

9 1 Tennis is not as exciting as squash. / Tennis is less exciting than squash.
2 Naples is smaller than Rome. / Naples is not as big as Rome.
3 Finland is colder than Greece. / Greece is hotter than Finland.
4 Spanish is easier than Hungarian. / Hungarian is more difficult than Spanish.
5 Victoria is not nearly as friendly as Natasha. / Victoria is much less friendly than Natasha.
6 The hotel in Glasgow was much better than the hotel in Edinburgh. / The hotel in Edinburgh was not nearly as good as the hotel in Glasgow.
7 Fantasy films are much more exciting than romantic films. / Romantic films are much less exciting than fantasy films.
8 Cartoons are much funnier than detective films. / Detective films are much less funny than cartoons.

11 1 elegant, 2 aggressive, 3 dangerous, 4 poisonous, 5 cuddly, 6 furry, 7 stunning, 8 deadly, 9 cute

12 1 deadly, 2 cuddly, 3 furry, 4 stunning, 5 poisonous, 6 dangerous, 7 aggressive, 8 elegant

13 1 adorable, 2 attack, 3 defend, 4 poison, 5 frightening, 6 suppose, 7 stay, 8 agree

14 B **1** Because they eat older and dying fish and they keep the ocean clean from other dangerous fish.

Everyday English

1 Don't get me wrong, 2 I'm not sure, 3 I wouldn't think so, good point

UNIT 5

2 1 they had to go everywhere on foot. 2 enjoy the sights of London. 3 was really good.
4 F, 5 T, 6 F
7 She spent six hours shopping.
8 She wasn't sure if it was cool.
9 She liked the working machines and buttons best.

4 1 fiction, 2 fact, 3 fact, 4 fiction, 5 fiction, 6 fact, 7 fact, 8 fact

5 1 which c), 2 who c), 3 which a), 4 who b), 5 who c), 6 who a), 7 which a), 8 whose b), 9 whose c)

6 1 which, 2 who, 3 who, 4 whose, 5 which, 6 whose, 7 whose, 8 which, 9 who

7 1, 2, 3, 5, 8, 9

8 1 Spielberg is the man who made the film *Jurassic Park*. 2 Do you know the girl that lives upstairs? 3 Is this the bus which goes to Piccadilly Circus? 4 I've got a friend who lives in London. 5 Did you buy the T-shirt which you like so much? 6 Where's the woman who has the key to this door?

11 1 bridge, 2 art gallery, 3 buildings, 4 tower, 5 shopping centre, 6 shops, 7 park, 8 street, 9 square, 10 museum

12 1 park, 2 square, 3 bridge, 4 districts, 5 river, 6 stations, 7 art galleries, 8 street, 9 shops, 10 buildings; secret word: Paddington

13 B **1** She's really interested in Harry Potter.
2 Its → It's, thats → that's, photo's → photos, it's → its, cant → can't, wont → won't

Everyday English

1 There's a thought, it's worth a try, 2 In your dreams, 3 It's a deal

UNIT 6

2 1 like Maths, 2 about her party, 3 good mark, 4 made two wishes. 5 is a picture of her dog. 6 but Cathy hoped it wasn't as bad as she feared. 7 Because they got the results only on Monday. 8 It was the best party ever. 9 She did badly. / She got the worst result in the class.

4 1 T, 2 T, 3 F, 4 F, 5 F, 6 T, 7 T, 8 T, 9 F

5 1B, 2A, 3B, 4B, 5A, 6A

6 1 miss, will take, 2 don't eat, will get, 3 help, will give, 4 doesn't stop, will have, 5 will be, run, 6 will go, invite

7 1 What will you do if it rains at the weekend?
2 What programme will you watch if you turn on the TV tonight?
3 What will you eat if you feel hungry after dinner tonight?
4 Where will you go if you go away this weekend?
5 What will you play if you play sport this weekend?
6 Who will you talk to if you phone someone tonight?

8 1 he doesn't speak to me for a week. 2 she doesn't take me to school when it rains, 3 he doesn't give me money, 4 she doesn't let me use the computer, 5 he doesn't play football with me, 6 he doesn't go for a walk with me

9 1 I won't help him with his work unless he asks me to.
2 He won't phone me unless it's very important.
3 He will be sick unless he stops eating.
4 There will not be a party unless you study for the test.
5 You will be late unless you run.
6 Mary won't have to go there unless she wants to.
7 He won't speak unless you speak to him first.

10 **1** 1 Yes, I am. Very. 2 Well, for example, I never walk under a ladder. 3 Because it'll bring me bad luck, of course.
2 1 No, not at all. 2 I just don't. I think we make our own luck. 3 No, I don't. I think they're silly.

11 1 will bring, 2 will you make, 3 come, 4 make/made, 5 comes/came, 6 making, 7 will bring

12 3, 4, 5, 2, 1

13 5, 7, 1, 9, 11, 3, 10, 6, 4, 2, 8

15 B **1** She should phone Amy in the afternoon.

UNIT 7

1 She's wearing orange.

2 1 happy. 2 is allowed to wear make-up at school. 3 because of his name.
4 F, 5 F, 6 T
8 They have been friends for half a year.

4 1 friendship, 2 really good friends, 3 were little, 4 a long time, 5 weekends or only meet them at school, 6 everything, 7 your problems

5 3, 7, 5, 4, 8, 1, 6, 2

6 1 for, 2 since, 3 since, 4 for, 5 since, 6 for, 7 since, 8 for

8 for: a few weeks, a lifetime, many years, a few seconds, three days, a couple of hours
since: 1999, she was a child, this morning, last Friday, the weekend, 10 p.m.

9 1 has been, 2 's/has, worn, 3 've/have lived, 4 've/have known, 5 's/has had, 6 has liked, 7 has played, 8 've/have been

11 Dialogue 1
1 have, had, 2 've/have had, 3 have/do, used/use, 4 've/have used / use, 5 'm/am using

Dialogue 2
1 have, had, 2 've/have had, 3 have/do, used/use, 4 took, 5 Do, want

12 1 b) out, 2 a) up, 3 a) up, 4 c) mind, 5 c) stormed, 6 b) on

13 A2, B4, C5, D6, E1, F3

14 linke Spalte: 7, 4, 8, 6
rechte Spalte: 1, 2, 5, 3

15 1 matter, 2 alright, 3 bit, 4 Poor, 5 well, 6 just, 7 terrible, 8 rash, 9 awful

17 B **1** He should let her know how he is.

UNIT 8

2 1 F, 2 F, 3 T, 4 had a company that made guns and canons. 5 but she found acting boring. 6 not really successful. 7 It blocked the signals that guided the torpedoes. 8 Because they didn't believe she could be so intelligent. 9 They remember her as one of America's most important inventors.

4 1 machine, 2 alphabet for the, 3 to read and write, 4 talking leaves, 5 every word, 6 sentences, 7 the different sounds of the Cherokee language, 8 translated the bible, somebody published a Cherokee newspaper, 9 20,000 people speak

5 1 T, 2 F, 3 T, 4 T, 5 F, 6 T

6 2, 4, 5, 1, 6, 3

7 1 got, 2 met, 3 haven't met, 4 has just broken, 5 lost, 6 has just gone, 7 has already, 8 arrived

8 1 've/have always been, 2 invented, 3 've/have tried, 4 haven't / 've/have not had, 5 had, 6 came up, 7 've/have already tried, 8 worked/works, 9 's/has ever read

9 1 have, seen, 2 invented, 3 took/transported, 4 took/transported, 5 Has, thought, 6 has, seen, 7 answered/said, 8 answered/said, 9 didn't, watch

10 1 A Have, been, B went, A did, visit, B visited, had
2 A Have, met, B met, A did, say, B asked

12 1 invent, 2 discover, 3 design, 4 experiment, 5 improve, 6 produce

13 1 discovered, 2 invented, 3 worked out, 4 designed, 5 's/has experimented, 6 improved, 7 produces, 8 try it out, 9 find

14 Down: 1 experiment, 2 invent, 4 discover
Across: 3 produce, 5 improve, 6 try out, 7 design

15 B **1** There are more than 300,000 objects on four floors.

Everyday English
1 The sooner the better, 2 You're having me on, aren't you? 3 Leave it out, 4 more or less

UNIT 9

2 1 is 2.6 million, 2 mechanic and a nurse, 3 in the bush, 4 T, 5 F, 6 F, 7 He felt something pulling on their tent. 8 They went out of the tent and ran to the car. 9 They saw a big crocodile that was pulling the tent into the river.

4 José: Peru, Agripina: Bolivia, Renato: Brazil, Raukani: Venezuela

5 1 Raukani, 2 Agripina, 3 José, 4 Renato, 5 Raukani, 6 Renato, 7 José, 8 Agripina

6 1F, 2A, 3D, 4C, 5E, 6B

7 4, 5, 6, 2, 1, 3

9 5, 1, 3, 2, 6, 4

11 1 will not / won't be allowed, 2 will not / won't be allowed, 3 were not / weren't allowed, 4 were not / weren't allowed, 5 are/'re allowed, 6 be allowed

12 1 James is allowed to watch TV, but he isn't allowed to watch TV after 10 o'clock.
2 Sarah is allowed to go to bed late, but she isn't allowed to get up late.
3 We are allowed to wear jeans to school, but we aren't allowed to wear shorts.
4 They are allowed to listen to music, but they aren't allowed to listen without headphones.
5 I am allowed to go to my friend's house, but I am not allowed to stay for the night.
6 She is allowed to have parties at home, but she isn't allowed to play loud music.

13 1 James' parents let him watch TV but they don't let him watch it after 10 o'clock.
2 Sarah's dad lets her go to bed

late but he doesn't let her get up late.
3 The headmaster lets us wear jeans to school but he doesn't let us wear shorts.
4 Mum lets them listen to music but she doesn't let them listen without headphones.
5 Dad lets me go to my friend's house but he doesn't let me stay for the night.
6 Her parents let her have parties at home but they don't let her play loud music.

15 3, 6, 1, 5, 2, 4

16 dye your hair, get a tattoo, go roller-skating without pads, buy your own clothes, have a party at home, use your parents' camcorder, go to the disco, come home after ten at the weekend, turn your music up really loud, get a nose stud, play video games all day, watch TV after 10 o'clock, eat too many sweets

18 1 I could lend you some.
2 Why don't I ask my brother to lend you his.
3 Would you like me to come with you?
4 Do you want me to ask my mum if you can have it here?

19 1 Would you like me to come with you?
2 Why don't I ask my brother to lend you his.
3 Do you want me to ask my mum if you can have it here?
4 I could lend you some.

21 B **1** He can meet tomorrow afternoon.

UNIT 10

2 1 F, 2 F, 3 T
4 discussed what to do. 5 looks after a lab. 6 organised a protest. 7 He promised a meeting to sort it out. 8 He suggested that some of the older kids could be computer labbies for three hours every afternoon so that they can use the lab too.

4 three windows → a couple of doors, to change your mind → for a meeting, 2 years → 4 years, school library → sports field

5 1 Sue, 2 Jill, 3 Mark and Ron, 4 Joanna, 5 Lucy and Andy, 6 James

6 1 Lucy and Andy, 2 Sue, 3 Joanna, 4 Mark and Ron, 5 James, 6 Jill

7 1 won't be able, 2 wasn't able, 3 were allowed, 4 was able, 5 won't be allowed, 6 weren't able, 7 haven't been able

9 5, 7, 1, 3, 4, 2, 6

11 5, 3, 4, 2, 1

12 1 save, 2 locally produced, 3 plastic bags, 4 recycle, 5 litter bugs, 6 distances

13 1 He should buy locally produced apples. 2 She shouldn't leave rubbish on the beach. 3 He shouldn't drop litter in the streets. 4 She should recycle glass bottles. 5 He shouldn't take a plastic bag. / He should bring a basket. 6 She should save water.

14 B **1** The entry is free but they are happy for donations.

Everyday English
1 Guess what, I knew it, 2 Nice one, No chance

UNIT 11

2 1 F, 2 T, 3 F
4 the coast north, 5 north of San Francisco, 6 very friendly
7 Because the people there are very friendly.

4 Bay Bridge

5 1 spend time with family. 2 6, 3 because it always looks good in the films, 4 the view, 5 because there's lots of things to do there, 6 find her work at his company

6 a 2, b 1, c 3, d 4, e 6, f 8, g 7, h 5

7 3, 4, 5, 1, 6, 2

8 1 've/have been working, 2 've/have been talking, 3 've/have been waiting, 4 've/have been taking, 5 have, been learning, 6 Have, been living

9 1 wrong, 2 wrong, 3 right, 4 wrong, 5 right, 6 wrong, 7 right, 8 wrong

10 1 I have known Henry for three years.
2 We have been walking for hours and I'm tired.
4 We have had our dog since last year.
6 They're not at home because they have gone on holidays.
8 You got the answer to question 3 wrong.

11 1 Have you ridden, 2 've/have been walking, 3 Have you been, 4 've/have seen, 5 've/have been having, 6 Have you bought, 7 've/have been looking, 8 haven't found

12 1 backpack, 2 dirt road, 3 ridge, 4 canyon

13 1 dry, 2 signal, 3 spot, 4 canyon, 5 backpack, 6 ridge, 7 headquarters, 8 dirt

14 1 signal, 2 headquarters, 3 backpack, 4 dirt, 5 spot, 6 dry, 7 Canyon, ridge

15 1 f), 2 d), 3 e), 4 a), 5 g), 6 b), 7 c)

17 B **1** She wants to know if they get the ticket on the bus.

UNIT 12

2 1 a birthday party, 2 with their boat's motor, 3 turned the boat over
4 three of their children to swim to the nearest island. 5 for a boat to pass by. 6 because they needed drinking water.
7 They found plums and coconuts.
8 They stayed there for four days.

4 linke Spalte: 2, 7, 10, 3, 1, 6
rechte Spalte: 5, 9, 8, 4

5 10, 5, 6, 7, 1, 8, 2, 4, 9, 3

6 1 active, 2 passive, 3 passive, 4 active, 5 active, 6 active, 7 active, 8 passive, 9 active, 10 passive

7 1 is found, 2 are read, 3 are chosen, 4 are invited, 5 are asked, 6 is filmed, 7 are watched, 8 are asked, 9 are chosen

8 1 were woken, 2 was thrown, 3 was destroyed, 4 were damaged, 5 were broken, 6 was blocked, 7 were closed

9 1 were killed, 2 injured, 3 taken, 4 were treated, 5 was damaged, 6 was, destroyed, 7 were closed

10 forest fire, tsunami, drought, earthquake, mudslide, volcanic eruption, hurricane, avalanche

11 1 earthquake, 2 flood, 3 forest fire, 4 avalanche, 5 drought, 6 mudslide, 7 volcanic eruption, 8 hurricane

12 1 under, 2 away, 3 near, 4 under, 5 near, 6 away

13 1 earthquake, 2 cracks, 3 collapsed, 4 crushed, 5 escaped, 6 safe, 7 rescue

14 B **1** He put his rucksack too far away and it started sliding down.

Everyday English

1 It's up to you, 2 Just in case, Here you are, 3 Don't look at me

UNIT 13

1 A3, B6, C1, D4, E5, F2

2 1 (quite good) friends, 2 for Sandra, 3 so shocked
4 F, 5 F, 6 T
7 Because Jenny saw John at the cinema and didn't tell Sandra.
8 He said it was not Jenny's fault.

4 2, 3, 1

5 1 Ken, 2 Eve, 3 Eve, 4 Ken, 5 Ken, 6 Eve

7 4, 1, 6, 3, 5, 2

8 1, 7, 5, 3, 4, 2, 8, 6

9 1 no, 2 yes, 3 no, 4 no, 5 yes, 6 no

10 1 had, 2 went, 3 I'd get, 4 didn't, 5 had, 6 wouldn't, 7 would, 8 wouldn't

11 1 If I liked Sally, I'd talk to her. 2 If he had a computer, I'd send him emails. 3 If she wasn't ill, she'd be at school. 4 If I didn't like you, I wouldn't help you with your homework. 5 If they weren't on holiday, they would be here today. 6 If my modem wasn't broken, I'd surf the internet.

12 1 A What would you do if you lost your key? B I'd go to my friend's house.
2 A What would you do if you saw a famous person?
3 A What would you do if you saw your teacher at the school disco?
4 A What would you do if you were the headmaster of your school?

14 picks, nerd, group, cheeky, grounded, detention, weird, dilemma

15 1 grounded, 2 cheeky, 3 dilemma, 4 nerd, 5 detention, 6 picks, 7 weird, 8 group

16 1 by mistake, 2 deserve, trouble, 3 meet up, stay behind, 4 owe me, lent, 5 rude

18 B **1** Her wish is to have twelve butterflies that fly around or behind her.

UNIT 14

2 1 form the delta, 2 live there/in the delta, 3 July and August, 4 all have private showers and toilets. 5 there is a large dining room where you can take your meals. 6 stay in two different types of camps. 7 They have a breakfast and then the first drive of the day starts. 8 They can relax until five. 9 There is the second drive of the day at five.

4 1 reading and travelling, 2 He has written 17 books. 3 She is a detective. 4 She's a big lady and she's proud of herself and Botswana and she loves Africa. 5 She teaches us about everyday life, wildlife and the do's and don'ts in African society. 6 Because he was born in Zimbabwe.

5 1 Jonathan, 2 Maria, 3 Sid, 4 Hannah, 5 George, 6 Miriam, 7 Mike, 8 Anna

6 1 'm/am going to get, 2 'm/am going to find, 3 'm/am going to find, 4 'm/am going to earn, 5 'm/am going to put, 6 'm/am going to wait, 7 'm/am going to hear, 8 're/are going to fall, 9 'm/am going to wake, 10 'm/am going to make

7 1 're/are going to drive, 2 're/are going to see, 3 aren't going to go, 4 're/are going to stay, 5 's/is going to rent, 6 'm/am going to remind

8 1 're/are going to go, 2 're/are going to fly, 3 's/is going to meet, 4 're/are going to stay, 5 'm/am going to take, 6 'm/am going to use, 7 's/is going to be

9 1 What are you going to do at the weekend? 2 are you going to, 3 is going to, 4 aren't you / are you not going to, 5 are you going to

10 1 a) planned, 2 b) hired, 3 b) made, 4 a) found, 5 c) check, 6 c) look, 7 a) buy

11 find: out about good restaurants, information about the best beaches
book: a holiday, a trip
make: a trip, a hotel reservation
plan: a holiday, a trip
buy: a car, a dictionary, a map of the area
hire: a car
check: the area out on the web

12 3, 5, 1, 6, 2, 4

13 B **1** Alessia's parents are talking about moving.

Everyday English

1 a complete waste of time, 2 on my own, 3 A real pain, not the only one